FERGIE

MY LIFE
FROM THE CUBS
TO COOPERSTOWN

FERGIE

MY LIFE
FROM THE CUBS
TO COOPERSTOWN

Ferguson Jenkins

with Lew Freedman

TRIUMPH
BOOKS

Library of Congress Cataloging-in-Publication Data
Jenkins, Ferguson, 1943-
  Fergie : My life from the Cubs to Cooperstown / Ferguson Jenkins, with Lew Freedman.
    p. cm.
  Includes bibliographical references.
  ISBN 978-1-60078-171-1
  1. Jenkins, Ferguson, 1943- 2. Baseball players—United States—Biography. 3. African American baseball players—Biography. 4. Chicago Cubs (Baseball team) I. Freedman, Lew. II. Title.
  GV865.J38A3 2009
  796.357092–dc22
  [B]

                                                                              2008050289

This book is available in quantity at special discounts for your group or organization. For further information, contact:

Triumph Books
542 South Dearborn Street
Suite 750
Chicago, Illinois 60605
(312) 939-3330
Fax (312) 663-3557

Printed in U.S.A.
ISBN: 978-1-60078-171-1
Design by Sue Knopf
Photos courtesy of Fergie Jenkins unless otherwise indicated

This book is dedicated to my mother,
Delores Louise Jenkins,
to my father, Ferguson Jenkins Sr.,
and to my children,
Kimberly, Kelly, Delores, and Raymond.

Contents

Foreword

When Ferguson Jenkins joined the Cubs, we became friends very quickly. We both enjoyed the outdoors, hunting and fishing when we were away from the ballpark. Fergie had a daughter, and my wife and I had four daughters, so our families became friends, too. I met his relatives from Canada and some of his other close friends back in Chatham.

Right from the start, we rode back and forth to Wrigley Field together from the Chicago suburbs and talked the whole time about baseball, fishing, and hunting. A lot of the other guys played golf, but I didn't, so I was glad to have somebody on the team who enjoyed the same hobbies I did. We got to know each other really well and hit it off right away.

When Fergie first came over to the Cubs from the Philadelphia Phillies in 1966, he was a bullpen pitcher. But Leo Durocher, our manager at the time, saw this tall, lanky guy, and Fergie showed Leo something that made him think he would be a good starting pitcher for us. So, the following year, he made Fergie a starter, and that changed things for the Cubs, for baseball, and for Fergie. It was the true beginning of his Hall of Fame career.

Fergie and I also enjoyed raising hunting dogs. We kept them at a friend's place in Barrington and went bird hunting there, a lot of pheasant hunting. We had a lot of good times together, in baseball and away from the ballpark. At one point, Fergie and I bought a boat together, a 25-foot Chris-Craft, and used it to fish on Lake Michigan.

We were just two young guys trying to pick something up to use for fun. But then we realized we had no place to park the boat. We found out that it was pretty hard to get a slip in one of the Chicago harbors on Lake Michigan. We called up the city, and they told us there was no room. We didn't know what to do. We needed a place for the boat. Then we called someone we knew, and I don't know what he did, but he might have told somebody it was two stars for the Chicago Cubs who needed space, because about six hours later someone called and said, "We found a slip for you."

Having Fergie on the team was a lot of fun for me because he liked to do some of the things I liked to do, but he was a great addition to the Cubs' pitching staff. Any time Fergie went out to the mound, it gave us a lot of confidence that we were going to win the ballgame that day. The numbers and records prove that. He didn't give up too many hits, and he didn't give up too many runs. Whenever he went to the mound, it reassured us that we were going to be in the ballgame. We knew he was going to pitch a good ballgame, and most likely he was going to win.

Fergie had control, and he had the pitches to get hitters out. Every now and then he would position his outfielders. He would turn his back to the plate and face me and put one hand over his navel, point his fingers, and tell me to move over a couple of feet. He had such control with his pitches that he was pretty sure where the ball would go when the hitters hit it. He put me closer to the foul line, and the ball would be hit there. Fergie was one of the only pitchers I knew who could do that.

For a period of time, Fergie and I had this thing going that when the season started we would each write down our goals, put them in an envelope, and put them away in our lockers. He would write down how many games he was going to win. They were goals we had for ourselves, and nobody knew what they were besides us.

A lot of Cubs players were together for several years in the 1960s, and we shared the 1969 season when we thought we were going to win the pennant. Guys like Ernie Banks, Ron Santo, Randy Hundley, Glenn Beckert, Don Kessinger, Fergie, and I became very close. We had great chemistry and spent a lot of time together. It was a case of a close-knit ballclub, and we enjoyed each other. There weren't two or three weeks that went by when we didn't congregate with all of our families. Our wives were together and talked. We have kept our friendships going for 40 years. Randy Hundley's fantasy baseball camps have had a lot to do with that. That brings a lot of us together every year.

Fergie has had some tragedies in his life, and when his wife Mary Anne was killed in that automobile crash, we had just come off a cruise together. Then when his little girl was killed, we all reached out to Fergie, called him on the phone to let him know we were thinking about him, and convinced him to come to Arizona for one of the fantasy camps when he otherwise would have stayed home. It was a chance for us to help him a little bit and boost his feelings.

When Fergie was going through those tragic moments, it was a good thing that we all congregated. We had a sit-down dinner, about 25 of us, and sat around and talked baseball. That was good therapy for Fergie. He has had some difficult times, but he has bounced back.

Fergie spends a lot of time doing charity work. He flies all over the country. Any athlete who appreciates what he has gained through playing professional sports is conscious of giving back, and Fergie does a lot. I really do admire what he's doing. He's doing a great job with it.

–Billy Williams
Hall of Fame 1987

Introduction

When a baseball fan mentions the name "Ferguson," everyone knows he is talking about Ferguson Jenkins. Ferguson is a more common last name than first name. The recognition factor is probably even higher if the name "Fergie" is uttered because that's Jenkins' nickname and his preferred method of identification.

Fergie is an informal name, and Jenkins is not a man who holds much with pretense. He is an informal guy who enjoys greeting people and estimates he has signed 1 million autographs over the last four and a half decades. If throwing a fastball 90 miles per hour did not leave him with any soreness in his right hand, arm, or shoulder, scrawling his signature should at least produce writer's cramp.

From the time he first adapted to pitching as a schoolboy in Chatham, Ontario, until he retired from Major League Baseball in 1983, Ferguson Jenkins was a marvel on the mound. He concluded a 19-year big-league career with the Philadelphia Phillies, Chicago Cubs, Texas Rangers, and Boston Red Sox, with 284 victories and 226 losses for a .557 winning percentage.

Jenkins won at least 20 games in a season six years in a row and seven times in eight years. He is one of an elite corps of pitchers to strike out more than 3,000 batters in a career, and his lifetime earned-run average was 3.34. Jenkins' longevity, productivity, and excellence earned him induction into the National Baseball Hall of Fame in 1991. He was the first Canadian citizen—and remains the only Canadian—so honored.

A tremendous athlete who excelled in a number of sports as a youngster—and remains an avid hunter, fisherman, and all-around outdoorsman as well as an active golfer—Jenkins channeled his skills into befuddling batters and achieving rare distinctions during his playing days.

Jenkins is a man of many parts. He was a Canadian in the United States' national pastime. He was a black man who overcame discrimination in the American South. He was the toast of big cities from Chicago to Dallas, but never forgot his small-town roots. He had a natural gift, but after retiring as a baseball player, he sought to teach pitching wizardry as a coach. Jenkins is a man who has reaped the financial benefits of being a famous athlete, but gives back to his communities—American and Canadian—with passionate fund-raising for good causes and makes himself available for events coast-to-coast in both countries to help others.

Jenkins has been a very fortunate man in many ways, but he has endured terrible personal tragedies and had his faith in God tested by them. There have been unforeseen challenges over the years that might have left another man bitter, but he has persevered. As there often is for anyone who lives long enough, there has been glory and heartbreak for Jenkins along the way.

Best remembered for his high-flying days with the Chicago Cubs (though he is also enshrined in the Texas Rangers' team Hall of Fame), Jenkins has fond memories (and stories from) each of his major-league clubs. With some, it was because of the success he enjoyed. With others, it was simply because of the good company—teammates—who contributed to making his stays tremendous fun.

Jenkins was a well-paid athlete for his time, but by modern standards he was underpaid. During Jenkins' prime pitching years in the 1960s and 1970s, the top salaries earned by superstars in baseball surpassed $100,000 but peaked out at Hank Aaron's $200,000-a-year contract.

Mixed in with his active travel and donation of his time for charitable work, including raising money for the Ferguson Jenkins Foundation (an Ontario-based organization that contributes to worthy groups in Canada and the United States), Jenkins also travels extensively, making personal appearances where he is one of the star attractions. And when the Cubs call, Jenkins is a willing vocalist, leading the singing of "Take Me Out to the Ballgame" during the seventh-inning stretch at Wrigley Field.

Few people are as much in need of a planner in their suitcase as Jenkins. If it's Tuesday, it must be a sports collectible store in Chicago on the Fergie itinerary. If it's Wednesday, it must be Cooperstown for a Hall of Fame event. If it's Thursday, it must be Kansas City for a golf tournament. To Jenkins, a handy calendar with commitments penciled in is as important as carrying his frequent flyer number in his wallet at all times. Have carry-on satchel, will go.

For a two-hour autograph appearance at a new store called the Fan's Edge in a Chicago suburb during the 2008 baseball season, Jenkins settled into a cushy armchair in front of a spare table and greeted a line of fans that extended most of the length of the store and out the door into the shopping mall corridor. The store sponsored Jenkins' appearance as part of its grand opening strategy, so the autographs were free to patrons.

Some of the fans were gray-haired, clearly old enough to have cheered for Jenkins when he pitched for the Cubs for the last time 25 years earlier. Some of the children accompanying parents or grandparents did not really know who he was, but were urged to pose for pictures with the Hall of Famer in hopes that they would appreciate the moment later, when they are older. Some were teenage boys who were sports memorabilia collectors wishing to add to their private stash of baseball souvenirs.

Jenkins keeps his head clean-shaven in Michael Jordan style ("I'm bald," he says), wears a small earring in his left ear, and for such casual public appearances dresses casually in shirts that do not require tucking into the slacks that are fancier than jeans, but less formal than dress pants. Each time Jenkins cupped a gleaming, naked white baseball before autographing it, he showed off his large hands. The combination of long fingers, wide palms, and the round ball demonstrated how he was able to so superbly control the baseball when he threw it past batters. It loomed larger than a golf ball in an average-sized hand, but could still just about be tucked out of sight.

Since Jenkins was only committed to a 120-minute session, the rule applied to those waiting was simple. Only one item signed at a time, but the fan could retreat to the end of the line and come through again. Given that many fans brought several balls, programs, photographs, or art pieces featuring Jenkins, that announcement was accompanied by an exhalation of relief.

It was apparent quite quickly that Jenkins was a veteran of the autograph-signing world. He was pleasant to everyone, heard out their private stories of prior contact with him or of watching him pitch, but smiled wider for the shy little kids who were just six, eight, or 10. He suspiciously eyed a trio of boys in their early teens and had them pegged as working for a dealer. Jenkins signed their stuff, but couldn't get them to admit they were anything but his most fervent admirers. They came through the line time after time, so he was positive they were being paid to show up. Jenkins was born in 1942, not yesterday, so he had observed such activity before.

"Hey, big fella, how are you?" Jenkins beamed at a four-year-old redheaded boy named Jeffrey.

Jeffrey, who no doubt did not comprehend the rules of engagement, pushed two Ferguson Jenkins baseball cards across the table.

"Okay," Jenkins said, signed both, then imparted a life lesson: "In girlfriends, one is good, and two is bad."

A little girl had two cards, too, but she held them tightly.

"Throw them down," Jenkins said gently. "I can't sign them in your hand. I could sign your hand. I've done that a few times."

A father urged a son to ask Jenkins to sign a ball on the sweet spot. This momentarily confused Jenkins. So many years after first picking up a baseball, he was still searching for a sweet spot, more commonly mentioned in connection with a bat.

"If the ball was sweet, I would have won 500 games," Jenkins said.

Jenkins offered a mix of charm and assembly-line efficiency to keep the line moving. He was asked the largest number of autographs he had ever signed in a day.

"I did 5,000 balls one day between 9:00 AM and 6:00 PM," Jenkins said. "I did 500 T-shirts with people holding them up."

That was the closest he ever came to being forced onto the disabled list for autograph signing.

When a fan, clearly a discerning baseball card collector, dropped a Ferguson Jenkins rookie card on the table, the player paused, picked it up, stared at his younger self from 1966, and laughed. Rookie cards of Hall of Famers and other stars have been hot collectibles for the last decade or so, but Jenkins' rookie card is unusual.

It was issued by the Topps Chewing Gum Co. at a time when the firm placed two young prospects on one card. So Jenkins shares his Phillies rookie card with another Phillies farm system player named Billy Sorrell. Considerably lesser known than Jenkins, Sorrell did play parts of three seasons in the majors with the Phillies, Giants, and Kansas City Royals. His experience in the big-time amounted to 85 games, primarily at third base. Sorrell had a lifetime average of .267. Jenkins remembers the player who never made it as big as he did and admits the irony that Sorrell's autograph is much rarer than his.

"If you want to get Billy Sorrell," Jenkins said, "you have to go to San Diego."

Unlike many stars asked for their autograph who demonstrate the penmanship of a doctor writing a prescription, Jenkins' signature, on flat or curved items, is quite clean and decipherable.

"Years of practice," Jenkins said. "I just think if you're going to write your name, you should make it legible."

One teenager who did not know Jenkins' signature habits requested that he write "Hall of Fame" next to his name. Jenkins, as do most of those elected to the Baseball Hall of Fame, writes "HOF" and the year of his selection with his autographs.

"Young man," Jenkins said with a laugh, "I put that on everything but checks."

One fan handed Jenkins a baseball he had previously signed in 1994. The signature was fading. So Jenkins signed it a second time. Another fan brought a Cubs commemorative automobile license plate featuring team Hall of Famers Ernie Banks, Billy Williams, Ryne

Sandberg, and Jenkins. Banks had already signed it, and the guy was going after all four. Jenkins added his name.

Many people went through the line repeatedly. A pair of middle-aged women with gray hair, who professed to be long-time Jenkins fans, said they were getting their Christmas shopping done early by having him autograph balls, jerseys, and the like. It was going to be a very Fergie Christmas at their house.

One of Jenkins' last customers of the day surprised him. A very enthusiastic woman who had been a Cubs fan essentially since birth, according to her explanation, handed Jenkins a present. It was a ticket to the National Baseball Hall of Fame induction events of July 21, 1991. That was the day Jenkins went into the Hall, and since he got in free that day, as did his family and closest friends, he had never seen the official tickets.

The gift was sincerely appreciated. However, when she invited Jenkins to dinner at her home that night with her husband and child, he chose to decline. It seemed like an offer to chuckle over, but it didn't matter. Jenkins was on the go. He was scheduled to fly out of Chicago the next morning for his next gig being Ferguson Jenkins. There were miles to fly and charities to help. The journey that began in Chatham, Ontario, in 1942 is ongoing.

–Lew Freedman

1

Hall of Fame

The day I was inducted into the Baseball Hall of Fame in July 1991 was a very special day. I had my kids with me on that hot day, and my father was there. My dad was 86 years old and in a wheelchair. He could walk, but he didn't have much energy, so he used the wheelchair for mobility. My father, also named Ferguson Jenkins, was the happiest one in Cooperstown. He sat in the front row of the spectators, and when I was giving my induction speech, I looked down at him a couple of times.

Dad used to take me to the ballpark as a kid and to the hockey arena. My dad played in the Negro Leagues of Canada when he was younger. He played on a team called the Black Panthers one year, and the next year it was called the Chatham Black All-Stars.

It was great to have my father and kids there. But my mother had passed away by then, and it was an even more emotional time for me because my second wife had died only months earlier. They announce the names of those selected for the Hall of Fame in January and then have the actual event in Cooperstown in the summer.

The day before the final vote for the Hall of Fame class of 1991, I got a phone call from Jack Lang, the secretary of the Baseball Writers of America organization that administers the voting. He told me that it looked as if I was one of the leading candidates.

I was definitely following the process. I had been on the ballot already. I had become eligible five years after retiring in 1983. Gaylord Perry, who won more than 300 games, was also eligible. And so was Johnny Bench, the Cincinnati Reds' catcher. They took Bench and Carl Yastrzemski before us. The next year I thought I might have a shot because Gaylord and I were the two winningest pitchers on the ballot. They took Jim Palmer and Joe Morgan.

Gaylord and I were pretty close. We had played together in Texas with the Rangers. We wondered if we might go into the Hall of Fame together. After Palmer was elected, Gaylord called me up, and he was ticked. "How in the hell can they take Jim Palmer?" he said. "I won 314 games, and he only won 268." And I had 284. I said, "Gaylord, don't worry about it. Next year, 1991, it will be us. You know 1991 could be our year."

I was pretty confident it was going to happen. People were telling me all the time, "Fergie, with your records and all the games you won, you'll be one of the top guys on the ballot."

Jack Lang called back and informed me I had been selected for the Hall of Fame. The announcement was made in mid-January, and they wanted me to get on a plane to New York for a press conference. I phoned my father and said, "Dad, I'm in the Hall of Fame." He was so happy.

Once you get that phone call, you know you are perceived as one of the best. The Hall of Fame is a distinct class of athlete in any sport. In my own mind, I knew I was a good ballplayer. But now I was considered one of the best for sure. Whenever I have made appearances since being inducted, I try to conduct myself as a Hall of Famer. I feel like I am representing more than myself—I am representing a class of people. It's a class of people who played the game to the utmost of their ability and are considered the upper echelon of their sport.

It was shortly after the announcement that my wife Mary Anne passed away from pneumonia, brought on by injuries she suffered in a bad car accident. So it became a sad thing wrapped up all around the Hall of Fame. We had a daughter together, and she had a son, Raymond, whom I had adopted.

Months later, the Hall of Fame put the inductees up in the Otesaga Hotel, the famous old hotel in Cooperstown. The morning of the induction ceremony I got up early, played golf, then went back to the hotel room, and just stayed there memorizing my speech. I had written out the highlights on a memo pad. I kind of did it as a reminder so I wouldn't leave out any of the people who helped me in baseball.

I mentioned the scouts and the different coaches who helped me throughout my early years of baseball in Canada. Our system is a little bit different than the system in the United States. The Canadian system starts with Tyke and then you move along to Bantam, Pee Wee, Midget, Juvenile, and Junior. Junior is where I started to pitch, where the players were 15 and 16.

A little later, I started playing with older players because of my ability. I was pretty much on their standard even though I was younger, but believe me, I was pretty raw. I fit in because I was a tall kid. If you look up my record in the *Baseball Encyclopedia*, it says I was 6'5" when I played in the majors. But I was already at least 6'4" when I was in my mid-teens. Everyone thought I was older because I was such a big kid.

In Cooperstown, I was in my own room, looking for some quiet time to reflect and to prepare. My father and the kids were in another room with a friend of mine, who was helping to take care of the kids. I just wanted to be isolated for an hour, even if it meant going into the bathroom and locking the door.

The Hall of Fame induction attracts thousands of people, and Cooperstown is a small town. They have moved the ceremony all over the place. Sometimes they have it in a big field. The year before I was inducted, they held it outdoors. It rained and got muddy, so they had to bring it inside to an auditorium. My year, they planned to use the auditorium. I was inducted with Gaylord and Rod Carew, the great Minnesota Twins' hitter. Also, the family of Tony Lazzeri, the former Yankee, was there, and the family of the White Sox owner, Bill Veeck. There were some other individuals being inducted into the media wing for newspaper and radio work. It was a large stage.

That particular day, there were three countries represented with living players. Rod Carew is from Panama. Gaylord is from the United

States, and I am from Canada. I didn't see any Canadian flags, but when they announced my name, all of a sudden a band from Chatham began playing the Canadian national anthem. My theme song when I came into Cubs games at Wrigley Field was "Canadian Sunset." Playing the national anthem in Cooperstown was more moving for me.

I was pretty proud of being inducted into the Hall of Fame and having my dad there. I'd accomplished that for him first. It was also special to be the first Canadian in the Baseball Hall of Fame. There are a lot more Canadians playing in the majors now, but there weren't too many when I was playing. What was nice was that a lot of the people who had been involved in my life were in the audience, including some of my coaches from my youth. That day my dad was just proud of me. I could see it in his face and when we wheeled him around town.

When I spoke, I tried to mention teammates who were important to me and instrumental managers and coaches who helped me improve as a pitcher. And I mentioned the four teams I played on. I also mentioned Mr. Wrigley—Philip K. Wrigley—the owner of the Cubs for so many years, and Tom Yawkey, the owner of the Boston Red Sox.

Then I got to my father, and I looked at him. When I mentioned my mother, Delores Jenkins, I choked up for about five seconds. My mother had never seen me play baseball because she was blind. She went blind while giving birth to me. She had been to some games and listened to games on a transistor radio all the time. After I made the majors, my mom came to some games in Chicago, Cincinnati, and Pittsburgh, I think.

She told me that when she was in the crowd and had her radio going with the ear piece in, she could tell how I was doing from the radio announcer's commentary and by how the fans reacted. She got a good sense of the games in that respect. She was happiest when I won, of course.

Induction day in Cooperstown was broiling. It was hot plus. But they did the media interviews with the radio and TV people first. Rod Carew, Gaylord, and I were all sitting in a line. Gaylord had on a green suit with a white shirt, and he was literally soaking wet. He asked me why I wasn't nervous. I said it felt like Opening Day. I had a lot of enthusiasm. I always had a lot of adrenaline flowing when I pitched Opening Day—and I had a lot of Opening Days in Chicago.

Rod Carew got up, but he didn't speak very long. He looked incredibly hot. He was wearing a blue sport coat and gray pants, and the back of his pant legs were soaking wet. (When I got up later, I said, "Rod's got to be a little nervous. Look how he's sweating.") At the end of his speech, Rod kind of delivered an interesting thunderbolt. Indicating heaven, Rod said that Billy Martin had to be up there watching or listening. Billy Martin had coached all three of us, Rod with Minnesota, and me and Gaylord in Texas.

Then it was my turn. I was so cool, calm, and collected. I had rehearsed and memorized my speech. They announced my name, da-da-da-da-da. When I came up on the stage, I was holding onto the plaque they gave me, and I completely forgot what I was going to say. It went completely out of my head. People were taking pictures, the Canadian national anthem was playing, but as soon as I handed the plaque back to whomever was there, I knew what I wanted to say, and I had it. Luckily, I brought the notes from the memo pad with me in my suit jacket. I put them right on the podium and ran right through the speech.

It was a pretty special day, as an athlete, for my father, and for Canada. I still have my Canadian citizenship. Chatham, Ontario, was my home, and it will always be my home. It is located about 50 miles from Detroit.

When I look back at growing up in Chatham, it was a great place for kids. I never had any problems, and there were no pressures playing sports in school. I was very, very fortunate. You look at kids who play sports now, and there is always something. Maybe they're pushed to do this or to do that by their parents or coaches. A lot of people embraced what I was doing.

I grew up in an ethnic neighborhood. There were Japanese, Polish, Dutch, and black people. But I grew up Canadian. We were all Canadians. There was no race discrimination. We were all the same. Nobody cared if you were black or not. We were all friends.

5

The only time I really felt discrimination for being black was when I first signed with the Philadelphia Phillies and started out in the minors. Before that, I barely had an inkling about discrimination against blacks. I had never lived it. I read in the newspaper about how blacks couldn't eat wherever they wanted to in the American South, about how they couldn't go some places, and they had to be careful what they did and what they said. When I signed my contract, I said, "Man, this is great. I'm a professional ballplayer." That's the first step in the dream for everybody.

It has been years since I was inducted into the Hall of Fame, but I never forget that day. It comes up often in conversation. People see me at public appearances and ask what my feelings were that day and how it changed my life. Being a member of the Baseball Hall of Fame does change your life. Every time induction day comes up, you think about it again, what a special moment it was.

The Hall of Fame ceremony is really part of a weekend. On the Thursday, when I first got there, practically nobody recognized me walking around town. I was just getting acclimated to the situation. Friday, things were a little more hectic. Saturday was totally different, and Sunday was off the charts. Everybody was going, "Oh, you're Ferguson Jenkins." On the Thursday, I went to the drugstore to get some toothpaste, and when I got back to the Otesaga Hotel, there were the credentials, my identity card, so to speak. Once you get to golf on Saturday, they want you to wear them, and then on Sunday. In essence, those four days kind of change your life.

I've done something that I'm very, very proud of. I'm very proud of being in the Hall of Fame for my sport. I did some good things in the game. The game was good to me. I try to be good back to the game. I try to tell people that all the time when I make appearances. Many players who do card shows or personal appearances act like they're being punished because they're there. But they have already taken the promoter's money. People want to see you as a former famous ballplayer, and you have agreed. Some guys feel they're being used after they already have said they would make the appearance. I've heard a lot of guys don't really act nice.

I've had some fathers come up to me with their sons and their own fathers, three generations, and say, "Hey, we've seen you pitch." Or a young couple, where one of them says, "My dad took me to my first ballgame, and I saw you pitch at Wrigley Field." It's nice to hear that.

Being chosen for the Baseball Hall of Fame absolutely changed my life. I think it did so in two ways. One was my thinking personally about what my performance was all about when I played, and the other was a sort of stamp of approval, a validation by others. I thought I was a good ballplayer, and then they told me I was a good ballplayer.

I did some good things in the game with the Cubs, the Rangers, with Boston. When I played, I did not make enough money in baseball to live off of the rest of my life, so I still have to make some money. I make the appearances to make money. Being a member of the Hall of Fame allows me to charge more money for an appearance, but at the same time I am not like other guys I hear about who won't go anywhere unless it's $25,000 or $30,000. I don't want to break anyone's budget. I'll go for what they can afford. The fact that I am a Hall of Famer puts me in a higher echelon. The people who ask me to come and make an appearance will get a Hall of Famer.

I enjoy meeting people. Maybe I do it more than other guys, and that's factored into it. I like the fans. I only played two years in Boston, but I still get a lot of memorabilia sent to me from Boston fans. I made an appearance just next to Boston in Cambridge, and I didn't think the line was ever going to stop.

I have been a Hall of Famer since 1991, and it's still enlightening to me that people recognize me for what my accomplishments were in baseball. Whenever I sign an autograph, people always ask, "Can you put 'Hall of Fame' down?" I put it down all of the time because I earned it. It's nice to say you're now a baseball Hall of Famer and couple it with your signature.

Being a member of the Hall of Fame stays with you. It stays with you until you pass. I think of some of the oldest Hall of Famers, like Bobby Doerr, who turned 90 in 2008, and Bob Feller, who is only a few months younger than Doerr, enjoy putting down "HOF" after their names, and I like it, too.

I also wear my Hall of Fame ring a lot. Some guys get it and put it away and never wear it in public. Gaylord Perry and I made a promise to one another that if we earned Hall of Fame rings we would wear them, and we decorated them the same way. The Hall of Fame rings all look similar. They have a platinum ball; they have "National Baseball Hall of Fame," your name, the position you played, and the day you were inducted engraved on them; and they have crossed bats and the front of the old Hall of Fame building. Gaylord put a diamond in his, and so did I. Whenever I do an event, I wear the ring.

Most guys don't wear theirs. Every time I go to a Hall of Fame induction, I tell the new inductees that they should be proud to wear their ring. Some guys take their World Series rings off and wear Hall of Fame rings. I know Johnny Bench doesn't wear his ring. But Ernie Banks wears his ring, as does Billy Williams.

I wear mine proudly. It's a pinky ring. People look at it and say, "Oh, that's a Hall of Fame ring." I say, "Yep." It's not gaudy. It's not big. It's just significant. It tells you, "Baseball Hall of Fame." And it means something to me, and that's why I wear it all the time.

Almost the moment I left the stage I began to reflect on what being a member of the Baseball Hall of Fame meant. Ted Williams was there, and 50 years had passed since he hit .406. Joe DiMaggio was there. Willie Mays, Ernie Banks, Duke Snider were all there. I thought, *I'm with the best ballplayers that ever put on a uniform, by far the best.* We were all in one room before going on stage, and after, when we were all on a bus going back to the hotel. I just thought, *Now you're in the Hall of Fame. It's definitely real.* The ceremony was over. Now I was a Hall of Famer. The whole world had seen it. I even had proof on a video-cassette of the ceremony.

I've never had a conversation with anybody since that day about being in the Hall of Fame that I didn't think about being with a select group of people.

2

Growing Up in Chatham: Choosing a Sport

Baseball? Hockey? Basketball?

At one time or another during my youth, I thought about trying to be a professional athlete in each of those sports. I think I made the right decision choosing baseball. Who knows what would have happened in my life if I had become a rare black hockey player? Or if my career had taken me to the NBA instead of into baseball?

Growing up in Chatham, Ontario, which had about 22,000 people, I was introduced to sports by my father, Ferguson Holmes Jenkins, whose nickname was "Hershey," like the candy bar.

Chatham is a hockey community like every town in Canada. I was introduced to hockey at about five years of age when my dad bought me my first pair of skates. Hockey is the national sport, and everyone starts very young, almost as soon as they can pull their own pants on. In Ontario, everyone plays hockey in the winter. My birthday is December 13, and the timing must have been just right in dad's mind to buy me some skates.

My father started me in baseball a little bit later, when I was seven or eight years old. At one time, my dad had a job where he worked for the distributor that owned a sugar beet factory, and he traveled a lot. That took him to Florida, and he saw a lot of spring training games, especially those with the Brooklyn Dodgers. But my dad's primary vocation was working as a chef. He was a great cook. I can cook pretty well, and I learned it from him. But he made fancy dishes in restaurants and sometimes at home. He was the chef at the local Holiday Inn.

Just a few blocks away from our home at 213 Adelaide Street was Stirling Park, where kids played baseball. It was named after Mayor Stirling, and there was a Stirling Dry Goods store just opposite the ballpark. My dad used to take me to Stirling Park and hit grounders and fly balls to me. That broke me in. The park was close enough to ride my bike there. Then I signed up for the Tyke baseball in the Sprucedale section of town, like Little League in the United States. Sprucedale was on the other side of town from our home, and there was a complex of fields, maybe six really small ballparks, for kids who loved to play baseball.

As a youngster, I was tall for my age, and when I signed up for baseball I became a first baseman. The coaches put the tall, skinny kid on first. My dad got me a first baseman's glove, and I started to learn a position and understand how the position fit into the game plan.

I liked baseball, but I also liked spending time with my dad. We had that time together at the ballpark. I was an only child, so I wasn't competing for attention, but he had to work, too. We had an older vehicle, and I remember riding to the fields with him. Windsor, Ontario, just across the border from Detroit, was only an hour away, and Ontario Steel was there. We lived in a blue-collar area. Ontario Steel was linked to Chrysler. The bumper department was there. They made frames for automobiles.

There was a lot of industry. But there were also a lot of farmers. The land outside the industrial area was all farms. There were companies that processed seed corn, wheat, and soybeans. It was an area with a lot of hard-working individuals.

When I started playing baseball, all of the teams were sponsored by local businesses or service organizations like the Kiwanis, the Jaycees, and the Rotary Club. They put their names on the backs of the uniforms—we were walking billboards. The groups paid the bills so kids could play ball. I was not a star player right away. When I was eight or nine and playing first base, I was just an average kid playing baseball. I was struggling like everybody else.

That began to change when I was 12. I had become a better athlete. I was kind of growing into my body, long and lean. By the time I went to high school at 14, I was already 6'2" or so. But I was very skinny. The other kids gave me the nickname "Plywood." I was really thin. Luckily, that nickname didn't stay with me for the rest of my athletic career. You could say that I outgrew it by gaining weight. Eating my dad's pastries and home-baked breads, pies, and pancakes, it was a wonder that I remained skinny as long as I did.

I always liked school, but to me sports and school were intertwined. They were connected for me because each year in school I learned a new sport. Everyone who is at all athletic in Canada plays some hockey. My dad helped steer me into baseball. Then, because I was tall, I started playing basketball. I also gravitated to the track team. I just enjoyed going to school and being involved in sports.

Since Chatham was a pretty small town, the same group of us played on the sports teams together. We became friends and we stayed friends. When I think back to the baseball teams of my youth, I remember all of the good times I had with Jack Howe, Mac Cundle, and Ken Montague. We played together and we won a lot together.

The first championship I experienced was with the Bantam level baseball team. That was probably age 12. We won two championships in the early 1950s. At the end of the baseball season, teams at a higher level could expand their rosters and bring up other kids. We were always graduating from our previous league to a higher league for the playoffs.

Turning 14 was kind of a watershed year for me. That's when I first started to think about playing sports professionally. It wasn't because I was such a great athlete, but the idea sprung from going to my first National Hockey League game and my first major-league baseball game. What I saw provided inspiration.

The hockey game was probably an exhibition because it was in London, Ontario. The Toronto Maple Leafs played the Boston Bruins, and one of the players on the Bruins was Willie O'Ree. Willie O'Ree was the first black hockey player in the history of the NHL. He was proving it could be done on the highest level.

11

Canada was—and is—a hockey-mad country. I was playing hockey, and there were other black players around. Seeing Willie O'Ree play in the NHL at a time when there were only six teams made me think. I said, *Man, I like hockey.* It seemed I was one of the better hockey players where I lived. I thought maybe that was going to be my ticket.

Hockey was huge in Chatham. I don't know if Americans truly comprehend how big hockey is in Canada. There are more Canadian baseball players and a lot of basketball players competing in U.S. colleges now. But back then it was almost all hockey. Actually, I'm sure for some older fans hockey is still all that counts. *Hockey Night in Canada* is a pretty special event.

I played hockey more than any other sport when I was kid. I'd say it was three or four nights a week at one point. My goal was to play junior hockey with the Chatham Maroons, but that didn't work out. My favorite team was the Montreal Canadiens, not the Toronto Maple Leafs, who were closer in Ontario, and not the Detroit Red Wings, the closest team of all. I guess it was because the Canadiens were so great. They were loaded with Hall of Famers and seemed to win the Stanley Cup every year. We always watched *Hockey Night in Canada* on the Canadian Broadcasting Company (CBC), the New York Rangers against Montreal, Detroit against Montreal, the Chicago Blackhawks, the Boston Bruins, and Toronto. That was the whole league back then. Even though the National Hockey League has grown to 30 teams, my rooting interest still focuses on the Original Six.

The Canadiens had so many great players, like Rocket Richard. But my hero was Doug Harvey, the defenseman. I also liked Edmonton later when they had Wayne Gretzky, and I like what the Pittsburgh Penguins are building now with Sidney Crosby. I still follow hockey. I watched the Red Wings, but I cared about the Canadiens. The Red Wings did have Ted Lindsay, Terry Sawchuk, and Gordie Howe, and those guys loved to play.

I tell people all the time that Derek Sanderson, who became a star with the Boston Bruins, was a pretty good baseball player in Niagara Falls. I played against him. He was a center fielder.

I really loved hockey, basketball, and baseball. I only played two and a half or three months of basketball a year. It was over quickly. I nearly reached my full height of 6'5" while I was in high school and wondered about becoming a forward in pro ball. For a while, I thought if I kept growing to 6'10" I would definitely be a basketball player.

During the summer when I was 14, my dad took me to my first major-league baseball game in Detroit. The Tigers were playing the Cleveland Indians, and one of the Indians' players was Larry Doby. Everyone knows that Jackie Robinson broke the color line in major-league baseball when he came up to the Brooklyn Dodgers in 1947, but not everybody remembers that Larry Doby joined the Indians only a few months later and broke the color line in the American League.

In the game that I saw with my dad, Larry Doby hit two home runs. I was struck by how the fans cheered him. That was the first time I had seen a player from a visiting ballclub get cheered by the Detroit Tiger fans. That didn't happen on the games I watched on TV. That made a big impression on me. I told my father, "You know, Dad, I think I want to play baseball."

It never crossed my mind that you never really heard about Canadians playing major-league baseball. There were only a few here and there that I ran into in the minors, or who had brief careers in the majors. When I went to the States, it was unusual to run across another Canadian. There was a pitcher named Ron Piche, who was from Verdun, Quebec. He played for six years in the majors starting in 1960. Johnny Upham, who was from Windsor, played a couple of years for the Cubs, and we played together in Little Rock, Arkansas. Billy Atkinson, who came along later and played for the Montreal Expos, was also from Chatham. Reggie Cleveland, a good pitcher from Swift Current, Saskatchewan, won 105 games in his career. We were teammates with the Red Sox.

Baseball has changed a lot in Canada since I was a kid. So many kids are playing the game. And there have been other really good players in recent years, like Larry Walker, who was a great hitter. He won three batting titles and had a .314 lifetime average. He probably would be rated the next best Canadian player behind me. The scouts follow the kids more closely, especially out West, and they have summer teams in places like Kelowna, British Columbia, that play good competition.

Players go to U.S. colleges to be seen. To get exposed they go to places where baseball is bigger. In Ontario they only play about 35 or 40 games in a season. I think by the end of the 2007 season, there were between 25 and 30 Canadian kids on the expanded 40-man major-league rosters.

When I was a teenager I did not understand what it took to become a major-league player. My exposure to that level of play was limited. I had mostly played in the summers just to play. All of my friends played. At that point I was also still a first baseman. I could hit pretty well, and I loved to go to the plate.

I didn't start pitching until I was 15. Pitching fit my concept of being an all-around player who could do anything. I was big and I could get the ball over the plate. I just threw the ball really hard and didn't give up a lot of hits. Come to think of it, that's not a bad basic formula for pitching success anywhere. I didn't know very much about how to pitch, though. I was not polished.

My coach with the Bantam team was Casey Maynard, who lived next door. It was under Coach Maynard's supervision that I made the shift to the pitching mound. One of my other hobbies as a youth was raising pigeons. Sometimes the pigeons escaped their roosts and alighted on Coach Maynard's roof. If Coach Maynard didn't feel he had my undivided attention, he sometimes jokingly threatened to make a dinner out of pigeon pie. At least I thought it was a joke. Coach Maynard, who came to my Hall of Fame induction ceremony, told people he thought I could play any position on the field. I don't know if that was literally true or not. It was true enough for Bantam level, probably.

There was not a lot of advance planning when I made my first pitching start for Coach Maynard. I was pretty well set at first base. I knew I had a strong arm, but our main regular pitcher was my friend Jack Howe. Jack came up with a sore arm, and I volunteered to pitch. I thought it would be fun to try it. It was a league game, and I was successful. To this day I don't know how I did it without practicing or preparing. I liked it. Being the pitcher meant you were a little bit more active than just standing at first base waiting for something to happen. It provided the feeling of being more a part of the game.

I started winning games. Jerry McCaffrey, who was an English teacher at John McGregor High School, had a friend who was an area scout in Windsor. Mr. McCaffrey, who has passed away, called his friend and told him about me.

The scout didn't come down until the winter when I was busy playing hockey. At that time I was a Doug Harvey defenseman wannabe. There weren't too many 6'5" defensemen in the NHL. The scout came up to me and said, "I hear that you're a pitcher." I said, "Well, not really, but I'm learning." That's how I met the Philadelphia Phillies' area scout Gene Dziadura, who became such a big influence in my life. Gene asked me to go over to a high school in Chatham and throw to him. It was a Tuesday evening, a weekday in the winter. Nobody was around. He watched me throw in the gymnasium. At 15, I really was raw and crude. So he taught me a better windup right there.

My dad was a good baseball player. He made $35 a week playing semipro ball decades ago, but never claimed he was good enough for the majors. He was not a large man. He stood 5'9". Most of my height must have come from my mother's side of the family. My mom, Delores, was 5'10", and the men on her side of the family were tall. As a teenager I was basically a big, strong guy who threw it hard enough to blow it past guys who were just regular high school players.

Pretty much all I had was a fastball. I toyed around with what I called a curveball, but it didn't curve very much. Sometimes I threw it as a curve and it turned into a fastball. I didn't learn how to throw a slider until I was playing winter ball in 1963. So it was not as if I had a huge repertoire of weapons in my pitching arsenal.

One huge thing I did have going in my favor from then on was my friendship with Gene Dziadura, who many years later also attended my Hall of Fame ceremony in Cooperstown. Gene was the main reason I wanted to do more with pitching. He thought pitcher would be my best position if I turned pro.

3

Family

I was born on December 13, 1942. My mother, Delores Louise Jenkins, had a difficult labor, and she became almost totally blind due to the delivery. It was a very unusual circumstance. Her struggles during childbirth ruptured her optic nerves. I was an only child, but I was a child who had great, loving parents.

My mother might have been my biggest fan, but it was not because she was a baseball fan. She was a fan of me. I was playing all of those sports, and my mother always made sure my uniforms were clean. My mom grew up in Chatham—her maiden name was Jackson—and my dad grew up in Windsor. He came to Chatham to play baseball and stayed because of my mom. He was playing for the Chatham Black All-Stars, and they were a good team.

Dad weighed 165 or 170 pounds. He was a center fielder and a good hitter, but he was not a home-run hitter. My mother had brothers who were 6'1" and 6'2". Her grandparents had come north on the Underground Railroad. Her ancestors were slaves in Kentucky, where her grandfather had worked on a plantation. My grandfather on my mother's side was tall, very thin, and dark-skinned. My grandmother was lighter-skinned.

My mom enjoyed my playing sports. She always wanted me to participate. She had very, very poor sight, so in essence she could never really see me play. She wore glasses, but they didn't help very much. She walked using a white cane. My mom had some peripheral vision that enabled her to watch TV a little bit, but she was legally blind.

When we went places like family picnics at the nearby lakes, she would use her white cane, but my grandmother, Cassie Jackson, who lived with us, came along. We basically had to hold mom's hand. A little bit later in life, when she was in her forties, my mother took up bowling. She was pretty good at it. This was five-pin bowling. My mother was right-handed, and what they did at the alleys was put up a rail along the side. My mother would walk along the rail, feel the rail and then let the ball go. I can't remember exactly, but she had a pretty high average. It was over 150.

My mother was the most courageous person I've known. She was blind, but she did not let it deter her in the least from doing whatever she wanted to do. When my mother was a teenager, she played piano and was an avid swimmer. I always wondered if that was where her appreciation of sports came from. But those were two activities she had to forego because of her disability. It has been written often that if someone loses their sight, they tend to compensate for it by sharper development of other senses. That was definitely evidenced with my mother. She honed her sense of smell and feeling and hearing. People who did not know her could spend hours in my mother's presence without realizing she was blind. My father always had good jobs, either as a chef, or as a chauffer for rich people, so there was no financial pressure on my mother to work outside of the home. My mother enjoyed being a housewife, the cooking and cleaning. She might have been blind, but if I moved the furniture at all, or left things out of place, she knew right away.

Inside or outside, my mother was an active woman. She didn't want people feeling sorry for her because she was blind. She was independent and tried to take care of everything on her own. Not only did my mom have great pride, she instilled that in me and emphasized we should have great pride in our heritage. We had a Bible in the house that was five generations old, and the names of our relatives were in that book.

My father's ancestors came to Canada from Barbados, and they were fishermen. I once took a trip to Barbados and looked up "Jenkins" in the phone book, but there seemed to be 300 of them, so I didn't make any headway finding relations. I don't know precisely why my branch of the family moved north, or exactly when. They were fishing because they needed the food, but both my dad and I loved to fish for fun. I still do.

The story of how the Jacksons, my mother's family, came to Canada, was better documented. My ancestors were definitely slaves. They escaped from slavery in the American South before the Civil War, they said. My grandfather Jackson was very old, and I was very young, when he pointed out scars on his wrists and said he had been chained up at night. He recounted stories of how the family had come north with the help of white abolitionists and traveled by night to elude capture. I was young at the time and believed every word he told me, but I figured out later he was born too late to be involved in those events. I think he was telling the stories in the first person to make them more dramatic, but they were true stories that happened to his father or other families like ours.

When we studied history in the public schools, we never heard stories like my grandfather told. My first wife, Kathy, who grew up in Dresden, near Chatham, had a similar family history. One of the ancestors on her mother's side was Josiah Henson. It is said that Henson was used as the model for the hero in Harriet Beecher Stowe's *Uncle Tom's Cabin*.

Being a black Canadian made me very unusual when I began pitching in the United States in the 1960s. Chatham was a virtually prejudice-free environment. Canada was not so deeply infected by racism as the United States. I was aware of being black, but I never dwelled on it. I just was black, like my other friends were white. Or Japanese, in the case of Bobby Tsakimayasa.

Everyone got along and worked together in Chatham. It was not until my last year of high school on a road trip to Northern Ontario where there were few black people that I encountered my first hint of racism. We were on a baseball road trip when someone in the stands shouted "nigger!" at me. But there really was no conflict in my childhood, either in the household, or in the community. I was lucky to grow up where I did and in the way I did.

My mom never saw me succeed in sports, but she was aware of it. The newspaper printed stories about the games, and friends read them to her. There was word of mouth from people she knew. They told her all about what I was doing, so she knew I was a pretty good athlete. A lot of times she brought up how I performed in a game.

At no time did my mom ever say she wished she could see so she could watch me perform in a sporting event. She never came to the hockey rink in Chatham when I was playing. But when I was playing baseball in Chatham she went because she liked to sit outside. My dad and other friends sat with her when I was pitching, and they told her what was happening in the game. Later on my dad bought mom her transistor radio so she could listen to major-league broadcasts.

When I was growing up, the word used to describe black people was "Negro." My mother always taught me to be proud. "You're Negro, son, you stay Negro," she said. One time when I came home to visit her, I had grown my hair out in the Afro style, so it was all bushy and thick. She rubbed my head and asked, "What's that?" I told her it was the current style, but she was having none of that. She ordered me to get my hair cut, and I did.

To tell the truth, one reason my hope for a professional hockey career got sidetracked was my mother's attitude toward that sport. I came home from a game with 14 stitches in my forehead, and my lips and eyebrows cut. She said, "You're going to get banged up so I won't know you." She said that was the end of hockey for me.

The timing coincided with my improvement in basketball, so I didn't mind so much. I scored 45 points in a school game, and that made headlines in the local newspapers. At age 16 I was invited to play for a team with adults. Even though I was playing against guys in their twenties, I kept scoring between 15 and 20 points per game. That encouraged me to think about my potential as a pro basketball player. When I stopped growing, I realized I could never be a pivot man in the NBA at 6'5". I finally started to see baseball as my best sport.

In school I never truly ranked my favorite sports. It waxed and waned depending on what was going on in my life. When I was eight years old, my mother bought me a sports magazine, and I became enamored of the colored picture on the cover of pitcher Curt Simmons. I didn't know who Curt Simmons was at the time, but he had a very fine,

20-year major-league career, winning 193 games. The thing that most attracted me about that picture was his beautiful, colorful Philadelphia Phillies uniform. I looked at that picture for a long time and said, "I want a suit like that."

Although it was years before I became a pitcher, I always practiced throwing things for accuracy. Terry's Coal and Ice Yard was near our home, and a railroad spur ran up to the plant. Sometimes, when the freight trains were rolling past, I stood a fair distance away and threw rocks at the cars' open doors. I got pretty good at it. I really do believe that what sounded like a silly game helped me develop pitching control. For a bigger challenge, I tried to throw the rocks between the narrower spaces separating the moving boxcars. I could do that, too.

I was not always an innocent, though I didn't have any evil intent. When I was in elementary school, I sometimes hit rocks with a softball bat and broke windows at Queen Mary School. That earned me a visit to the principal's office.

As most kids do, I got into trouble making poor decisions that were risky. My friends and I acquired pigeons by grabbing them as they roosted under the neighborhood railroad trestle. We climbed hand over hand under the trestle, along a beam nine inches wide, and shined a flashlight into the birds' eyes. That paralyzed them for a minute, and we threw a net over them. Sometimes a train passed overhead while we were capturing the birds. The first time it happened it scared the devil out of me. The power of the train shook the entire trestle. We were lucky no one lost his grip and fell to his death.

Another time I climbed a tree to retrieve a soccer ball that had become lodged on a high branch. I rescued the ball but fell to the ground and broke one wrist while spraining the other. Doctors put casts on both arms for six weeks. The restrictions on my activities pained me more than the injuries.

Besides sports at McGregor High School and Chatham Vocational School, I also participated in square dancing and sang. I think when I lead "Take Me Out to the Ballgame" at Wrigley Field, I do a passable job. My singing background mostly stems from involvement in the church choir at the two churches we attended when I was young.

When we lived on Colborn Street near the ice plant, we attended AME Baptist Church. When we moved to Adelaide Street, we shifted our worship site to William Street Baptist Church because it was closer. We went to church every Sunday, and I continued that practice well into adulthood. I believe in the brotherhood of man under God, and I believe if all people believed in God and followed the teachings of the Lord, the world would be a better place and we could solve many of mankind's problems.

Maybe it was because she only had one child—me—and she didn't work outside the home, my mother loved it when my friends came over to the house. It was like having a house full of children for her. There were always snacks around like lemon pie and chicken, so my house became my friends' central meeting point. Eating pie at my house was an attraction, but for some reason we went through a phase where we threw pies into one another's faces as a practical joke.

When we had group sleepovers, we camped out in my backyard. We played poker, and my mom played with us. She was like the momma for the whole group. Despite being blind, my mom was so familiar with my best friends, she could recognize them when they came to the house or on the street even before they spoke. My friends were always amazed by that. We called ourselves "the Adelaide Street Gang." It sounded cool, but we weren't a gang of troublemakers. We were a gang in the sense that we were a group of friends who liked to hang out together.

My mom gave my friends love-life advice, too. If one of my buddies had a girlfriend he took home to meet his parents, he also brought the girl over to my house to meet my mom and dad. My mom had a big heart—they all wanted her approval.

I experienced an extremely harmonious childhood. Being an only child with a mother who had a disability—although she hardly acknowledged it—put extra responsibility on me at a young age, and I think I generally lived up to it.

In terms of academic achievement, I was not a Rhodes Scholar. I did well enough in school, never having a problem with failing grades, and I did love to read. I really enjoyed good stories. *Tom Sawyer* was one of my favorites. And I liked any story with an animal theme, like *Black*

Beauty, or *The Yearling*, or *Lassie*. I loved dogs. I had a mixed Labrador retriever–cocker spaniel named Tony when I was 11, a gift from my dad. Later in life I raised hunting dogs.

I live in Arizona now, but I remain a Canadian citizen. I am not going to give up my Canadian citizenship. I visit Chatham and other parts of Canada many times each year. Chatham is the place where I grew up, and I have fond memories of it. I still have a lot of friends there, and Chatham has always been proud of me. When I first hit it big, the residents of Chatham put up a sign reading, "The Home of Ferguson Jenkins." I am proud of that, and they are right. Chatham is the home of Ferguson Jenkins. Two of my daughters live there. And a lot of my good memories live on in Chatham.

When I say Chatham has always been good to me, that is true in so many ways. In 1967 the Chicago Cubs named me as the starting pitcher for Opening Day. I was warming up in the bullpen, and all of a sudden I heard my name called. My mom and dad were sitting in the stands waving to me. Ernie Miller, who wrote for the *London* (Ontario) *Free Press*, had arranged for them to come. They came from Chatham and went through Windsor to Detroit, where they caught a train to Chicago, to surprise me. It was pretty emotional. I was happy to see them. I waved to them, but I didn't go over until after the game because I was getting ready to pitch.

I pitched a complete game and beat the Phillies 4–2. The team photographer came out after the game and took a picture of me with my family. My mom said she listened to the entire game on the radio. The commentators had been kind to me on the air, saying a lot of good things about me as a first-year Cubs player, so that made her feel good. None of that would have happened without the Ontario newspaper.

Chatham would be more of a home now than it is if my parents were still living, but they have both passed away. My dad lived long enough to see me inducted into the Hall of Fame, but my mom did not.

My mother died at age 54 on her wedding anniversary in 1970 from stomach cancer. The main thing I found out about her when she died was that I did not lose a mother, I lost a friend, a counselor, a teacher, a person who was there whenever I needed her.

4

Preparing for Pro Ball

I was such a raw beginner of a pitcher when Gene Dziadura first saw me throw in that gym that he had to teach me a proper, efficient windup. I was just winding up my own way from watching guys and throwing. Gene became one of the most important people in my life, and we remain close friends. And that's even after I almost killed him with a pitch that knocked him off his seat on an overturned bucket.

Without Gene's help and guidance, it is hard to imagine that I would have become a major-league pitcher. I definitely would not have signed with the Phillies, and I don't know how my career would have started.

Right after he first saw me throw, Gene had the Phillies send a pitching instructional book. It showed how to hold runners on base, how to deliver certain pitches, and really how to become a pitcher and not just a thrower. There is a difference. Anybody can be a thrower, but it takes smarts to become a pitcher. Who would ever have guessed back then that I would eventually write my own baseball instructional book called *Inside Pitching*?

Over a period of several weeks, I went over that book and worked on everything in it. Gene kept working with me, too. In that way, the Phillies were my tutors. I worked out every Tuesday and Thursday on the fundamentals in the instruction book. It got me into a routine, and the book really taught me what pitching is all about. I was also still quite skinny, so there was no doubt I had to get stronger. Back in the late 1950s and early 1960s, nobody in baseball lifted weights. The theory was that you would become muscle-bound, and it would mess up your pitching. The only people who lifted weights were body-builders. You saw their pictures on the backs of comic books. Now if any coach or scout tells a young pitcher to get stronger, it's understood that means you have to hit the gym to lift weights.

My father had a really good friend named Andy Harding, a local policeman. He and his two brothers played baseball with my dad. They came up with the idea for me to chop wood to build strength in my shoulders. We didn't have a fireplace, so we didn't need wood cut for our use. However, after talking to Andy Harding, my dad bought an axe. He knew some people who lived in the country and got some logs dropped off in the backyard. Then he said, "Go to work." I set to the task of chopping big pieces of wood into smaller pieces of wood, turning them into kindling.

All I did was lift that axe up, swing it over my head, and crash it into the wood. I pulled the axe out and did it again. In the course of the month, just repeating the action over and over, I started to get stronger. My shoulders were getting bigger, rounded. After a little while, I started to like what I was doing, too, but the main purpose was being accomplished. That program definitely worked.

Later on we got a three-pound sledgehammer, and I smashed it down on things. For a while I just wound up and smacked that hammer down onto the pillows on the couch. My mom got tired of that pretty quickly and suggested I take my act outside to the front porch. It was a different striking motion than the axe, and it helped develop my wrists. That way I could throw a sharper curveball without tiring. These were old-time techniques. I remember seeing an old photograph of Babe Ruth chopping wood.

In winter I was very busy. I played hockey, plus a little bit of basketball, and on Tuesday and Thursday nights I pitched. The routines of wood chopping and wielding that sledgehammer really built me up. I adapted to the motions, and it became second nature for me to throw a ball properly and to throw it where I wanted by twisting my wrist.

Gene Dziadura built a contraption out of badminton standards for me to use to sharpen my accuracy. He set up the stanchions and roped them off, cutting a square in the middle of the netting. I threw balls to him. We were working on my location, but in those days nobody used that word to describe their pitching accuracy.

The idea was to throw between the lines, and I got pretty good at it. I could throw nine out of 10 into the square. Then he moved the strings around in the square to different spots, so the pitches were not all just right down the middle of the plate. He would have me hit spots. I threw a pitch over here for a strike and a pitch over there for the outside corner. One time he missed catching a pitch, and it hit him hard in a bad spot, let's say. I knocked him off his seat. I had the winter to work on these techniques, and the next baseball season I was a pitcher–first baseman, not a first baseman–pitcher. I had turned 16, and I was bigger and stronger, too.

My first game pitching had been a casual thing. I said I would do it, the coach said he knew I threw hard, so what the heck? I wasn't facing sophisticated hitters who were on their way to Cooperstown on a jet plane, but in the seven-inning game, I allowed just two hits and struck out 15 players. That's how my career was redefined. I still played the field when I wasn't pitching, and I liked to hit, but I became a member of the regular rotation.

The next season I was playing with the same group of guys. My teammates were Jack Howe, Matt Cundle, Dennis Roebuck, Larry Myers, Ken Montague, and a few other guys, and we were good. But the baseball season in Ontario was short. We only played 15 to 25 games. That meant I only pitched seven or eight games. The rest of the time I played the field and hit .400 my senior year.

I started to pay a little bit more attention to major-league baseball, but we didn't have a television set at the time. I liked the Detroit Tigers because they were close and the Cleveland Indians because they had Larry Doby. My strongest sports rooting interest still revolved around the National Hockey League and the Canadiens.

Major-league baseball in the United States—these were the days before the Montreal Expos or the Toronto Blue Jays—was out there, but I didn't follow box scores day-to-day. I was a devoted collector of baseball cards, however. I remember being happy to unwrap the packages and get a Mickey Mantle card, a Jackie Robinson, a Robin Roberts, or

Willie Mays. If someone had alighted on my front doorstep one night and whispered in my ear that one day I would be a member of the Baseball Hall of Fame with those very players, I would have insisted they were lying. My favorite card was of Ernie Banks of the Chicago Cubs. I never dreamed one day I would be Ernie Banks's roommate on the road.

I still enjoy looking at baseball cards. When I sign autographs at card shows, I sometimes make the rounds and look at the new cards. I have saved many cards over the years of players I liked or knew. And I have quite a few Fergie Jenkins cards, too.

My dad took me to Tigers games when he could. I never did become a particular fan of individual players, but I was aware of players on the team like Al Kaline and Charlie Maxwell and Frank Lary. I just cheered for the Tigers as a team. I was aware that Jackie Robinson of the Dodgers was the first black player to get into the majors, and I knew about Larry Doby. But the Tigers didn't have a black player yet. Ozzie Virgil Sr., who was from the Dominican Republic, was the Tigers' first black player, but they didn't integrate until 1958. Except for the Red Sox, they were the last of the 16 teams to integrate.

I never thought about whether the Tigers had a black player or not, really, and I think that's because of where I was raised. There was just never an issue of race in my hometown. My schoolmates were very diverse. There were Jewish kids, Mexican kids. There were kids whose families came from everywhere. That definitely served me well later in life as I traveled, had experiences overseas, and met ballplayers from all parts of the world. It also meant that playing soccer wasn't foreign to us, and that you didn't have to be French to play hockey, even if some people in Quebec thought you did. My neighborhood was pretty nonchalant, and I think a lot of that was attributable to all of us being interested in playing sports.

As a youngster, you never think about such things, but when I got older and signed a professional contract, I took some time to think about the opportunity I had been given. I don't really know how great a baseball player my father could have been, but I do know the major-league doors would have been locked to him because he was black.

Every time I did something well in sports and every time I moved up in baseball to another classification and began playing well in the majors, my dad told me he was proud of me. Not every kid is lucky enough to have parents who tell them that even once, never mind all of the time. Those parents must not think about how much of a difference that can make in the life of a child, just knowing that someone out there loves them.

I later told my dad that I was playing for both of us. I think I first said that to him after my first year in the minors. My father had traveled through the South, so he knew what it was like. My career started in the low minors. I played in Class D ball, but moved up to Class A, briefly Double A, and then Triple A—in Miami, Chattanooga, and Little Rock. Dad followed my career as much as he could. He and my mom got descriptions from local newspapers, saved the articles, and pasted them all up in scrapbooks. Sometimes I collected the clippings and sent them to my dad. My parents ended up putting together 14 scrapbooks about my baseball career, and I have them to this day.

But while I was still in school, except for Gene Dziadura, the scouts who expressed interest in me saw me as a first baseman or outfielder. By then I thought of myself as a pitcher, however. By senior year in high school, I also knew Tony Lucadello. Tony was a regional scout who was higher up in the Phillies organization than Gene. He signed a lot of quality ballplayers over the years. Later there was a book written about his scouting life called *Prophet of the Sandlots.* Tony was quite a guy, and even though Gene was more hands-on with me, Tony clearly wanted to sign me for the Phillies.

Gene kept in constant contact. I look at Gene as the man whose interest provided me with the stepping stone to baseball. He constantly prodded me on and showed me how to improve myself. At first it was more clinical, as a scout, but then he became a friend. Gene didn't want me to develop Superman bulging muscles, but he thought some weight work would help me.

My senior year in high school, I made my own weights. There was a 10-pounder and a 25-pounder. I used them for fine-tuning, to keep the tone in my muscles. I used them for years, even carrying them on the road in my suitcase and breaking them out in hotel rooms.

Gene also believed in running. It's commonly believed that as pitchers age, the legs go weak first. Nowadays you can't drive down the street in any town in North America without seeing someone jogging. It might be an older man, a middle-aged woman, a teenager, or an adult with a dog. Everyone runs, and it seems as if everyone wants to run a 26.2-mile marathon. When I was a teenager, nobody ran. If you were running in the street, it meant you probably did something bad and the police were after you. The only people who trained for the Boston Marathon were college guys on track scholarships. Now most trainers agree that running is a solid foundation for competing in just about any sport.

Gene ran with me. We ran at night on the local golf course, and we didn't stop running during the cold and snowy Ontario winters. It was more conducive to dog-sled running than humans running. When we ran at a golf course or a park in the winter, we left the car running so we could jump right in and warm up. Some people think you have to be crazy to run in snow, but I liked it because it was harder. It was kind of like running in sand—good work for the legs. During one winter run on the golf course, Gene forgot where a sand trap was. Snow completely covered the trap, and Gene plunged into it up to his waist. I got a good laugh out of that.

The workouts Gene Dziadura and I began when I was in high school stayed on my schedule on home visits for the next two decades. Whenever I came to Chatham, we ran together.

I was always a good athlete. That was God-given ability, and I was lucky to have that in my genes. But it takes more than the gift of basic ability to become a success in any professional sport, whether it's hockey, basketball, or baseball. You have to work at it when you are young, you have to work at it when you are in the big leagues, and you have to work at it right up until the moment you retire. Being a professional athlete can offer fame and riches, but nothing is promised to you.

The hard work and dedication never stops if you want to stay in the majors. There are always younger players coming along who want to take your job. The only way for you to keep it, year after year, is to keep on working and keep on learning. I came to baseball a little bit later than American kids do, and I most definitely came to pitching at an older age than many. When I first began pitching, I had enough natural speed to overpower most of the high school players I faced. That was not true in professional leagues. If I had ever let myself slip and forgotten my work ethic, I could have washed out at any time. The three years Gene and Tony worked with me before I signed a professional contract opened my eyes to what it meant to do something well. Nobody could help you as much as you can help yourself.

One thing you learn over time, if it is not innate, is how to be a true competitor, to seek every advantage. You might like a certain hitter personally, but you also have to realize he is out to batter you into submission. It's his job to crush your best pitch and score runs. You can never ease up.

There are years in your career when you are in your physical prime, but those years might not match up precisely with your mental prime. You come into the majors all young and excited, with the vigor of youth and the natural tools that make you think you can strike out the world. But as you age, you gain experience and wisdom. That's how pitchers enjoy long careers. They catalogue in their heads all that they see when they are young, and they trot it out a little bit later when they are older. That's the only way to survive.

5

Turning Pro

Compared to the money that draft picks receive these days, when I signed with the Phillies in the spring of 1962 after graduating from high school, I was paid peanuts. Unsalted peanuts. But obviously things were cheaper nearly a half-century ago, and to me the most important thing was the opportunity to play professional baseball.

Gene Dziadura and Tony Lucadello helped me, and Tony brought the contract to Chatham to sign me. I received an $8,000 signing bonus, plus a minor league salary of $400 a month. That sounded like a lot of money to me at the time, even if it doesn't sound like a lot now. But I was off to play baseball with the hopes and dreams of making it to the majors, and I had two guys in my corner from the Phillies who felt I could make it.

I know big-name high school athletes hold press conferences these days when they are about to commit to a college or sign a contract. We did it differently. I had generated interest from other teams, but really there was no question that I was going to sign with Philadelphia after the way Gene and Tony had treated me. My father planned a special dinner for the family and for the scouts. My dad the chef prepared a nice meal, and we sat around talking throughout the evening. To show you how different our "signing ceremony" was from a multimedia show at a school gym, we ate by candlelight.

Everybody knew what we were there for, but my mother Delores still had some reluctance about letting her 18-year-old baby go off into the real world. I could have gone to college, too, which I think would have made her happy. Gene and Tony both told my parents, whom they knew well by that time, that this procedure of signing right out of high school and going straight into the minors was the best thing for my career. They promised that I wouldn't be rushed and I would be given every chance to succeed.

Tony lived in Ohio, and he drove to Chatham sign me. Tony was a great guy. He was Italian, short, about 5'7", and he wore a straw hat, a sport coat, and dark glasses. He was very distinctive, but he held himself in a stately manner. He was a little bit more formal than people might have thought at first.

Tony was a famous scout, and he signed a lot of good ballplayers. For the Phillies he signed Mike Schmidt, who became a Hall of Fame third baseman; Mickey Morandini; Alex Johnson, who won a batting title; Johnny Upham; Toby Harrah; Grant Jackson; and John Herrnstein, a lot of guys who made the majors. He was a great judge of talent. He had a good track record, so the Phillies trusted him and we could trust him that he knew what he was doing. I don't know what percentage of guys that scouts sign make it to the majors, but Tony's record spoke for itself.

That night my dad said, "Ferguson, if this is the life you want to live, go ahead and do it. Prove to yourself you are worth your salt." He also urged me to work hard at all times. That philosophy had been imparted to me by both of my parents for years, and I already had been working hard. I wasn't going to change. Late in the evening, the contract and the pens were brought out, and I signed. I was a Philadelphia Phillie. And as soon as the Phillies presented me with my bonus check, I turned the money over to my parents so they could pay off the mortgage on the house at 213 Adelaide Street.

In the months leading up to graduation, I knew I was going to be leaving town to play professional baseball. People talked about it. It was cool. Some of my friends, Dennis Roebuck and Larry Myers, were being looked at, too. I thought Dennis was by far the best ballplayer in our age group (he was two years older) in Chatham. He was being scouted by Detroit and Cleveland. We all rooted for one another to get a chance. The knowledge that we were going to be professional baseball players kind of made us big men around town, even if it didn't win us any girlfriends.

My dad didn't let me get a swelled head. He kept reiterating that if this is what I wanted to do then I had to do all the right things. My dad ran with me, too, sometimes. Once we ran on a golf course when it was 17 degrees, and I was thinking (not saying), *Who believed this was a good idea? I knew it wasn't me.* But I also knew I had to keep doing it.

The signing, which created newspaper headlines in Chatham, took place only a couple of days after I graduated from Chatham Vocational High School. The day after our special dinner, I packed, and my parents drove me to Detroit for a flight to Pennsylvania. No, I was not going directly to the Phillies. I was scheduled to start my career at Class A Williamsport, the community that is home to the Little League World Series. I was excited to embark on the beginning of my professional baseball career. Certainly, there was some sadness leaving my parents, but the adventure on the other end of the ride promised to be thrilling and worthwhile. I was ready to go. My mother understood all of that, as well, but that didn't stop her from crying when she said good-bye. Her parting words of advice were to not get into trouble, to always listen to my coaches, to make sure I got a lot of sleep, and to give my all to succeed.

Gene came to the airport in Detroit with us. Gene was still a pretty young guy and in good shape, and Tony had suggested that Gene sign a three-week contract to play shortstop in Williamsport. They needed a fill-in, and he could help ease my transition to the pros. Gene pointed out to Tony that he was getting married right in the middle of that time period, so he stayed home.

Flying from Detroit to Pittsburgh was the first airplane trip of my life, and it was an awful trip. We bounced around the sky like a basketball. I was scared and my ears became fully blocked. I was thrilled to touch down even though I couldn't hear a thing when a representative of the Williamsport club picked me up.

The official from the team got me registered at the Williamsport Hotel, and that night when the team returned from a road trip, I met my roommate, Tommy, and he met me. Tommy was white and he was shocked to discover that his new roommate was black. In 1962 white and black athletes did not room together. The United States had not yet reached that level of comfort with race.

"Who are you? What are you doing in this room?" were just about the first words out of Tommy's mouth. I told him I was his new roommate. He said, "They must have thought you were white because of your name." He figured the team would work it all out the next day at the ballpark. I was not the only black player on the team. There were several black guys, including Richie Haynes, Dick Edwards, and Bobby Sanders. There was also a guy who would become much better known as a star hitter and a Most Valuable Player award winner—Richie Allen.

The manager was Frank Lucchesi, who had a long career in baseball. He managed in the majors, including a stretch running the Phillies. When we met, it was clear he didn't know what to do with me. He said I was such a raw specimen that the Phillies weren't actually going to put me on the roster, but wanted me to absorb the pro baseball scene and throw some batting practice for a while.

My experience was so limited I didn't even realize that throwing batting practice meant I was supposed to let the batters hit the pitches. It is called *batting practice* for a reason. So I was throwing hard and striking people out. It drove the batters crazy, but they laughed at me. The next day the hitters got back at me with a practical joke in the locker room. I found my cleats nailed to the floor, my pants tied in knots and my socks cut up. There was a lot of curiosity about how I would handle this situation, whether or not I would blow up yelling, or if I would take it in stride. I kind of laughed along with everyone. I had to pay for new socks myself, but that was the only financial damage. In Class A baseball, teammates know nobody is making any money, and if they are going to play a trick on you, it's a pretty safe bet it won't be an expensive one. They can't afford equal retaliation.

The roommate situation got worked out swiftly. The black players shared an apartment, and I moved in with them. Our abode was a former electrical appliance store called The Lighthouse, as if it were a fancy condominium development. It wasn't. One unusual aspect of The Lighthouse's previous life was that if you flipped one switch, five or six lights went on at the same time. I slept on a roll-away bed. The glamorous life of a minor leaguer, huh?

Because he went on to the majors, I had more contact with Richie Allen, or Dick, as he preferred to be called later, than with the others. Richie was a little bit older than me, and he had a car. Sanders had a car. Haynes had a twin brother, and they were both signed by the Phillies, but they didn't make it.

I was getting stale. I only spent four weeks in Williamsport while Lucchesi studied my work habits and my pitching form, and the Phillies mulled over the appropriate place to send me. Later in his career, fairly or not, Richie Allen got a reputation as a moody guy who was hard to play with. There was no sign of that when we played in Williamsport. He was happy playing baseball, and he took good care of himself. Allen knew he wanted to make it to the majors and knew he had the talent. He didn't smoke or drink, and he slept a lot. He had a goal and a plan. He was like the rest of us, starting out with high hopes and putting everything into the game to get noticed by the team and promoted.

Although the Williamsport circumstances didn't last that long, I can't say I was happy going through a routine where I did all of my working out before a game, then had to change clothes and go sit in the stands to watch my team play. After about a month, Lucchesi took me aside for a talk. He told me my work habits showed him I wanted to be a professional and that what he saw of my skills indicated that I would make it as a major leaguer. He then said the Phillies were shipping me to Class D Miami, where I would be able to pitch for real. They were starting me at the bottom. They didn't have Class F leagues; guys' egos probably wouldn't have been able to take it. Class D was low enough in the alphabet. They eventually did away with the names of all minor league classifications that were lower than A. No Class B, C, or D anymore.

"You've got a chance to make a lot of money in this game if you work hard," Lucchesi told me. At the moment, I was making a minor leaguer's low salary of $400 per month before taxes, so the words "lot of money" could have meant just about anything. Lucchesi said he would rather have kept me in Williamsport. I don't know if he was saying that to make me feel good, or if he meant it. But the Phillies sent me out.

Class D ball did not translate to first class. I got my luggage and was waiting around baggage claim. Miami sent the clubhouse kid to the airport to give me a ride. They must have just told this kid he was supposed to go pick up Ferguson Jenkins. The kid might have called my name, but my ears were plugged from the flight.

So I sat around Allegheny Airlines bag claim. This kid walks around and walks around, and finally we make eye contact, and I said, "Are you waiting for a Ferguson Jenkins?" He said, "Yeah. Are you Ferguson Jenkins? I thought you were white."

The kid brought me to the old Miami Stadium, and the game was under way. He dropped me off, and I got into the clubhouse and left my luggage there. But there was no one around. It was the first or second inning, so I went back out and sat in the stands. I was still far from a streetwise kid, still so naïve after Williamsport that rather than tell the ticket-takers I was a new player, I bought a $2 ticket. Afterward, I went back to the clubhouse to meet my new manager, Andy Seminick, a 15-year veteran who spent most of his playing days with Philadelphia.

Seminick came up to me and said, "I'm glad to have you." This was the low minors, and all of the players were the same age. We were all young kids, fresh from home, hoping to move up.

Over the last period of time pitching high school in Chatham, I was pretty dominant. I had a good fastball, but there were no radar guns to measure my speed. I did throw the ball relatively hard, and I had a fair curveball. I had a much better mound awareness after working so hard at it on those Tuesday and Thursday winter nights in the gym. I played in some high school tournaments that gave me wider exposure. I pitched and played first base in tournaments in Ann Arbor, Michigan, and Detroit. I carried two gloves wherever I went. That's how I got some interest from scouts with the Pittsburgh Pirates, Boston Red Sox, Chicago Cubs, Chicago White Sox, Cincinnati Reds, and Detroit Tigers.

I had pretty good range at first base, I ran pretty good, and had some raw power. The ball kind of jumped off my bat. We didn't use wooden bats, though. We had aluminum bats. I came off as an athlete with potential. By then I had decided I was a pitcher. Being a professional first baseman was only in the back of my mind, maybe as a fallback.

The Phillies' interest in me had helped me. The scouts knew my family. They had shown me they cared about me, and we were loyal to them. I don't know exactly how much money I might have received from another team, but we felt the Phillies had shown us a lot already. Scouts from other teams never came to my house. I saw the Tigers' scout around once in a while at games, but no team thought of me as a budding superstar. When I played in games around Michigan, I could see the scouts in the stands, taking notes, carrying clipboards. Some of them came over to talk to me after the game. It was like they were interested in me, but only so far. They didn't have the personal touch the way Gene and Tony did representing the Phillies.

Some scouts did call the house and talk to my dad. Scouts said, "We'd like to watch him play some more. Where's he going to play next? Does he have a game in Windsor? Does he have a game in London?" But the scouts didn't come to Chatham. To most scouts, I was a prospect that might be worth developing. No one else took anywhere near the interest in me as Gene and Tony did. So choosing the Phillies was not a hard decision to make.

When I got to Miami to start my professional career, my baseball education began for real, and my life education, too, after experiencing a somewhat sheltered upbringing in Chatham.

The black players were assigned to live at the Sir John Hotel. It was located on Biscayne Boulevard, and it was the place where all of the black entertainers who came to Miami also stayed. It was later destroyed in riots over racial issues. The whole area got burnt down.

My roommates were Alex Johnson and Reno Garcia, an infielder from Cuba who later died of cancer. There were a few other black players staying in the hotel, including a guy from the Virgin Islands. None of us had cars, and the only way for us to get to the ballpark was to take the bus. We had the same routine. Go outside and wait for the bus, go to the ballpark early, work out with our regular routines, play a game, and come home.

We were all the same age, 18 or 19, just starting out, and when we went through all of the running, throwing, hitting, and fielding drills, I felt I was just as good as anyone else. Class D's whole season was about 75 games. In the beginning, it was like Williamsport. I would warm up and throw and never get into a game.

I complained, and Andy Seminick said, "Young man, be patient. You'll get your turn." There was nothing for me to do except be patient.

I spent 6–8 weeks in Miami in the Florida State League, and I won seven games. My earned-run average was great, like 0.90. Miami went by fast. We were conscious of the separation of the races there at that time and were always trying to be careful not to incite anything. But if you were black in the American South in 1962, trouble had a way of finding you, even if you were innocent of doing anything wrong. One day we were on a road trip, traveling by bus between Miami and St. Petersburg, and when it was time for lunch, I got off with all of the other players. I didn't even think about it, other than I was hungry. When I went up to the counter at the restaurant to order lunch, the waitress simply said, "We can't serve you." She turned away from me and began taking orders from the white players.

The whole thing caught me off guard. I sputtered and didn't say much. I just turned around and went back to the bus. The other seven or eight black players were still sitting on the bus. I hadn't noticed that none of them came inside with me. They suggested that I ask one of the white players to order for me and bring the food back to the bus.

Nothing like that had ever happened to me in Chatham, or anywhere else in Canada. I was more shocked than angry, but the other black players were veterans at receiving this type of treatment, and they made it clear they were bitter. It was humiliating. Some of the black players were Southerners, and they had dealt with this sort of racism their entire lives. The black players from Latin America like Garcia were more like me. They had not experienced this type of discrimination at home.

This was a regular occurrence on bus trips around Florida. In some places, the black players were allowed to get off the bus and go around to the back of the restaurant for food. We could actually sit down there.

Alex Johnson and I preferred to do that than stay on the bus, but some of the other blacks who were furious about the dehumanizing treatment wouldn't do it. "My money is as good as theirs," they said of the white players. "Why can't we walk in the front door? We have just as much of a right as they do to sit in the front of the restaurant." They were absolutely right, and it was terrible to be treated that way. But at that moment in history, there was no power around that could make that restaurant serve us in a normal manner. I think Alex and I got more for our money by being served in the back, but that didn't make it right, and that doesn't mean being ordered around like that unfairly didn't bother me.

The same policies held true at hotels in the cities all over Florida. When we arrived for a series, the white players went to one hotel and the black players were ushered off to the black area of town to special housing with local black families or at black-owned businesses. We stayed in private homes in St. Petersburg and in "colored" motels in other cities. We encountered the famous white and black separate washrooms that you see in photographs from that era. That was the most ridiculous thing I had ever seen. One major inconvenience for the black players on the Marlins when we were on the road was trying to get something to eat after a night game. Tampa, St. Petersburg, these were not tiny towns, but there were no 24-hour eateries open in the black parts of town. If we wanted to get anything to eat at 11:00 at night, we had to go to the bus station.

The United States was on the verge of change in 1962. The civil rights movement was about to blossom, or explode, in the South, and things would change for the better. But the people didn't seem ready yet. Once, in Tampa, I witnessed the type of vicious, ugly hatred I thought I would never see and that I will never forget seeing. I stumbled upon a demonstration of about 20 black youths. They were protesting, marching and carrying signs, about the black and white treatment in a local cafeteria. Some of the signs read, "Unfair to Blacks" and "Freedom Now."

The demonstrators, as I well knew from personal experience, had a beef. This was a peaceful demonstration, the type of protest encouraged by the Rev. Dr. Martin Luther King Jr. But all of a sudden a pack of white youths attacked the black protestors, dumping water on them and throwing rotten fruit and eggs at them. That shocking display could have been worse—and things did get worse in places around the South—when policemen clubbed peaceful black demonstrators and turned snarling dogs on them. At the time I mourned for both races, wondering why everyone did not live in racial harmony the way we had in Chatham.

I saw things in Miami involving human relations like that, that I would have been happy never to have seen, but I wasn't homesick. I was just playing ball and trying to do well. I was making my way in professional baseball. The league had teams in Fort Lauderdale, Tampa, St. Petersburg, and Palatka, too. That was the Palatka Cubs. They didn't have many people there. That was an old park, and it was dark. You couldn't see in that ballpark. A lot of the other parks were pretty high class. Fort Lauderdale was a spring training ballpark. So was Lakeland for the Tigers and the White Sox's park in Sarasota. Tampa had Cincinnati.

The Florida State League gave a lot of players their start. At that time, Bert Campaneris, who was a really good friend of mine, played for Daytona Beach. Jimmy Wynn was in Tampa. Tito Fuentes was in Lakeland. I made my professional baseball debut with the Marlins as a relief pitcher against Lakeland, and the first batter I faced was Fuentes, who later was a shortstop with the Giants. I pitched two innings.

Over those six weeks, I got more comfortable pitching. I was making a lot of transitions. I had moved out of my hometown. I was growing up by myself on the road. I was improving as a pitcher. All of these were important stages that I had to go through if I was going to become a major-league pitcher.

One thing that was great in Miami was receiving regular letters from Tony Lucadello. As a scout, his job was pretty much done when he signed me on the dotted line, but Tony didn't forget me. He was a faithful friend and remained one. I was one of "Tony's Boys," as they called the Phillies' players he signed, and that meant Tony maintained his interest in my progress. He wrote me a letter of encouragement every week, and I really appreciated that.

People think of Miami as a glamorous vacation paradise, but Miami was smaller and less developed in 1962. I was making just $400 a month and didn't have a car. I really wasn't in a position to live it up. Plus, there was hostility to black people. The team gave us the names of places we shouldn't go because of the racial tension. The Marlins didn't want us to go to Miami Beach. It didn't bother me. I didn't want to go there, anyway.

When I was a boy, there were restrictions, rules, from my parents and coaches and the school that sometimes stopped me from doing what I wanted to do. I looked at this somewhat the same way, but I didn't even want to go to Miami Beach. We didn't have the money, we didn't have the transportation, and we didn't want to go, so the black players pretty much hung around black neighborhoods. We played some basketball in our free time and did a little bit of shopping. We didn't gamble for money because none of us had any. We just played basketball and tried to survive the summer where we were.

A lot of the things that made an impression on me happened on road trips. Once, in Tampa, the black players stayed in an old night-club. It had been converted into a hotel, and Alex Johnson and I were roommates. Alex found a couple of bugs in his bed and spent the whole night trying to sleep in a chair. He would not go back into his bed. I didn't find anything in my bed, so I slept in it. Not exactly being in five-star accommodations, we couldn't call the concierge and complain about the situation.

Another time, for games in St. Petersburg, the black players slept in a funeral home. This was not an old funeral home, or a funeral home converted into a hotel. This was an active, working funeral home. It was just us and the dead bodies. No, we did not sleep in coffins. The funeral home was in a house, and the top part had its own apartment. The second floor is where they had the coffins and where the funerals were held. And below that was the mortician's area. I did not really like it there, but I wasn't scared.

On a trip to Palatka, where we stayed in black neighborhoods, they put us up in a hookers' hotel. The team had about five rooms, and in the rest of the hotel they rented rooms by the hour. We saw girls coming back and forth, back and forth. Cars were driving up and parking, and cars were driving away. Sometimes in the middle of the night, we got a knock on our doors, and some guy yelled, "Is Julie in there?" or, "Is Barbara in there?" I'd just yell back through the closed door, "No, wrong room, fella!" I never told my parents about that experience. Welcome to Class D baseball in Palatka, Florida.

There were so many times the black players couldn't eat in restaurants, and we had to have our white teammates buy hot dogs and hamburgers for us to eat on the bus. Sometimes it felt as if we lived on Trailways buses. Sarasota and St. Petersburg seemed particularly hostile to serving us. Nothing was ever said about the situation as an issue, about its being wrong, or its being unfair. It was just done. The white players did complain on our behalf to the manager, but he couldn't do anything about it. It was tough to threaten the restaurant owners about future business when they didn't really care and we had no alternative place to eat, unless everyone wanted to join us at the bus station.

The Florida State League didn't do anything about the situation, either. They could have. Every team had the same problem. Change didn't start coming until after 1964, when the Civil Rights Act was approved by Congress. By then I was gone.

Sometimes when the Marlins traveled on the buses, Alex and I shopped for food ahead of time. Alex used to carry a cooler. He put juices, milk, apples, and oranges in it. We'd eat that on the bus and supplement it with the meals we could get any way possible. We only got paid $2 per day for meal money, so we weren't going to be spending fancy, anyhow.

Twice on one long road trip I went in the front door, walked up to the counter, and asked if the black players could eat in the back, get food from the kitchen handed to us out the back door. That was the cook's area. And they did it. We were just happy to have something to eat, especially if we had to play that night.

This does not seem like the United States of the 2000s. It was cruel, but I just put up with it. I was glad it only lasted six weeks or so, though, before I got promoted. I pitched 65 innings for the Marlins—

and struck out 69 batters—and the Phillies jumped me all of the way up to Triple A Buffalo.

That was much better competition, and I even got a raise to $500 a month. I needed the money, too, because the players in Buffalo dressed much nicer than the teenagers in Miami. The players were older and had been around. I did a double-take when I realized I was going to be expected to wear a sport coat and a tie more often. That was not my usual wardrobe, and it hadn't mattered with the Marlins. There went most of the raise.

The joke the players had about my promotion from Class D to Triple A was that Miami played in a T-shirt league and Buffalo played in a silk tie league. Everyone was the same age in Miami, but Buffalo of the International League had many players that had been in the majors. Players like Dallas Green, Jim Frey, and Dick Ricketts had some major-league service and wanted to get back to the big-time. I was no longer just one of the boys. I was more like the new kid on the block, the youngest player on the team. That was definitely a vote of confidence from the Phillies, an indication that the organization felt I was a player on the rise, a young player with a future.

Moving me to Buffalo was a test, to see how I handled better competition. Over the season's last six weeks, I was able to absorb baseball in an environment that was the closest thing to the major leagues. However, once again most of my absorbing was done from the bench. I was only used in three games in Buffalo. I finished 1–1, but my earned-run average was a lousy 5.54.

My mom and dad made plans to meet me in Buffalo for a game because it was close to Chatham. Only the game got rained out, and we were all disappointed. I learned a lot about baseball and life my first year as a professional, and because I finished the season in Triple A, I thought that's where I was headed the next spring, just one step shy of the majors.

When I returned to Chatham for the winter, I had a lot of stories to tell.

6

Moving Up in the Minors, Winter Ball

At the urging of the Phillies and with Gene and Tony's input, I made a critical decision to play winter ball in Managua, Nicaragua, in 1962–1963. If it was difficult to leave home to play for the Phillies in Williamsport and Miami, it was 10 times as complicated for a just-turning-20 Fergie Jenkins to commit to playing baseball in a foreign country where I didn't speak the language.

My Spanish was about as proficient as my Russian when I first went to Nicaragua, but not only did my Spanish improve, so did my pitching know-how. What a terrific experience that was for me.

There is a tremendous history of major-league players competing in the off-season in the warm-weather climate of Puerto Rico, Venezuela, Cuba, and other Latin American countries. The players earn some money playing baseball instead of working at more routine jobs like selling cars or insurance. In the 1930s and 1940s, when black players were not welcome in the majors, the top stars always played the Latin American circuit.

Players like Satchel Paige, Josh Gibson, Cool Papa Bell, and Martin Dihigo were the rage in Latin America. The caliber of the games was probably better than some major-league games. In later years, Latin American stars in the majors were expected to go home in the off-season and put in an appearance where they grew up, whether it was Roberto Clemente or less famous players.

The Phillies had a working agreement with the Leon team in Nicaragua. It was difficult to limit my time with my parents in Chatham, but I sensed that playing winter ball could be very important. I was right. I went to Nicaragua to play for 10 weeks and pitched a one-hit shutout almost as soon as I got there.

When the Phillies said I was going to Central America, I had to get out a map. There was one other North American on my team: Harry "Suitcase" Simpson, a first-baseman who spent some time with the White Sox and four other teams. The teams were allowed two imports per team. We played often, but we stayed in Managua. There were two ballparks.

I flew from Miami to Managua, and the airport was quite different from your average American airport. There were gun turrets above the runway. Soldiers patrolled at the ballpark, and they carried machine guns when they walked across the dugout roof. My impression was that the show of force was for the fans. I thought maybe there was a revolution going on. Whenever they closed the post offices or the banks, there were armed guards out front. When we walked back to our hotel after a game, there was a soldier there. It was not a tense atmosphere, but soldiers were always present.

My Spanish was horrible. I had difficulty ordering meals. Gradually, I picked up key words, and that helped. The early going was a challenge, but my struggles were eased by Fernando Alvarez, who was in the Washington Senators' organization and shared a suite with me.

The unit of currency was the cordoba. It was 55 cordobas to the dollar, so I got stacks of money. Fernando, whom I called Freddie, said, "Don't leave your money in your hotel room. You will lose it." A trainer spoke English, and I always left my money with him during games. We got paid after games. Then I took my money to the bank and sent a money order home. I'd only live on so much.

There was a certain romance to the experience. I was on my own, picking up the language, and the girls were very pretty. One of the first times I went out with other players, we went to a house that I thought was a bar. I didn't have any idea what I was walking into. It was a house of ill repute, and as soon as the girls saw me, they started yelling, "Hey, American!" I was so naïve that I responded by saying, "No, I'm

Canadian." As if they cared. The guys looked at me. The girls started talking about money, and it was the price for more than a drinking companion. When the other players began disappearing upstairs with girls, I still didn't know what the deal was.

At no point did anyone clue me in, and all I did was sit at the bar drinking Coca-Cola until the other players reappeared and it was time to go home. Could anybody be more green than I was?

My Nicaraguan season lasted from October until the end of January. Stories have spread over the decades about how seriously Latin countries take their baseball. We have seen the development of star player after star player whose roots are in Latin America, but back in the 1960s there was a tremendous local pride in beating other nearby teams.

The Leon team finished second in the league that winter, but the fans seemed on the edge of hysteria much of the time. They beat drums and sang. When a player made an error, he was booed. When a pitcher got racked up, he was booed. When the team bus left the stadium, fans threw rocks and garbage as it pulled away. Those fans needed to chill a little bit. As passionate as the fans are at Wrigley Field or Fenway Park, nothing compares to upset Latin American fans venting their emotions.

One thing I wondered about in Nicaragua was how I would cope with heat and humidity. Ontario is a cool-weather climate, and our summers are mild. I was pleased to discover that the heat didn't bother me. I played in some pretty hot weather in the majors, especially with the Texas Rangers. It would be brutal to try to function in Texas in July without air-conditioning. But I never felt the heat much when I pitched. In fact, it was at about this stage of my career that I took to wearing a long-sleeved jersey under my uniform shirt whenever I took the mound, regardless of how hot it was. On a trip back to Chatham, I was riding bare-armed in a car with one elbow hanging out the window, when Gene Dziadura gave me a frown of disapproval. He said no matter what the circumstances, I should always keep my pitching arm warm. That's when I developed the habit of wearing long sleeves. I loved my stay in Nicaragua. I won seven out of eight games and gained confidence.

The Phillies showed belief in me by sending me a major-league contract that doubled my original monthly pay from $400 to $800. I was making $500 monthly in Buffalo at the end of my first season, however, and when I talked contract renewal with older players, they said, "Don't take the first offer, Fergie." They thought I might be able to talk general manager John Quinn out of an additional $100 a month.

Rather than sign right away, I called Quinn on the phone. I told him I appreciated his giving me a major-league contract, but I thought I might deserve a little bit more money. He didn't. Quinn was a dour-looking man, and when you talked to him, he got right to the point. "Jenkins," he said, "we are pleased with your progress, but you're young, you're inexperienced, and you've got a lot to learn yet. We've given you a pretty good raise, and I think it's sufficient. We're being fair with you."

I was no prize-winning debater or defense lawyer, and basically I thought what he said was true. So I signed the contract and sent it back.

We had spring training in Dade City, Florida, in 1963, and that was a rural place. It had dirt roads and those Spanish moss trees. They were pretty. There were only a few streetlights in the town. At night it was kind of eerie. We were put up in another black area instead of with white players. The area scouts and coaches did bed checks on us. They drove over to our neighborhood and knocked on our doors. This was a minor league camp.

Coming out of spring training in 1963, the Phillies started me out in Little Rock, Arkansas. But Little Rock was too crowded with pitchers, and they hardly used me. I got into four games in Arkansas and pitched just 10 innings.

They had rearranged the classifications, and Miami had become Class A. So back I went to Miami and back I went to the Sir John Hotel, although I was pitching against slightly better competition than I had seen the previous summer. There were some older players, and the Marlins had a full schedule.

The Sir John was a hopping place, and not just for ballplayers. The quality of entertainment seemed to improve from the year before, or maybe being a year older I just appreciated it more. I remember that James Brown, who was fabulous, Etta James, Jackie Wilson, Little Anthony and the Imperials, and Gary "U.S." Bonds did shows there. It was great. We came back from the ballpark after night games, and those entertainers were performing at our hotel. That was pretty good stuff.

I was getting older, but I didn't drink much. I had a few beers. We got into the shows for free because we lived in the hotel. It was a good thing because I couldn't afford the 10 bucks admission to each show. The shows didn't end until 1:00 or 2:00 AM. We didn't have any coaches at the black hotel telling us to go to bed. We'd get a live show and then go to our rooms.

When we got up to start the day, we walked down to a local restaurant to eat bacon and eggs and grits. That's where I had grits for the first time. It was like cream of wheat. They told me you have to put butter and pepper on it. I tried it and liked it that way.

I was a much more mature pitcher my second year in Miami. I pitched in 20 games and went 140 innings. There was much less reliance on relief pitchers at the time, and I averaged seven innings per game. I finished 12–5 with a 3.41 earned-run average and struck out 135 guys, almost one per inning.

My experience in Nicaragua had been so pleasurable that when it was suggested I return to winter ball, I was enthusiastic about going to Caguas in Puerto Rico. The Caguas manager was Frank Lucchesi, who was also working his way up the Phillies chain. I had a terrific season. I made the All-Star team, beat Luis Tiant with a two-hitter, and my earned-run average of 1.24 was a league record. Not every player on every roster was a major-league-caliber player or prospect. But Roberto Clemente, Orlando Cepeda, and Tony Oliva were just a few of the great hitters I faced. Lucchesi said he expected to see me playing in Triple A the next summer and that he had only heard good reports about me throughout the organization.

I spent three winters in Latin leagues, and I have no doubt that what I learned and experienced in those places helped develop me into a major-league pitcher more quickly than I would have otherwise.

In 1964 the Phillies brought me to Clearwater, Florida, for my first spring training with the big club at Jack Russell Stadium. I met Jim Bunning, Johnny Callison, Chris Short, and Art Mahaffey, some of the regulars on a very good Phillies team. That team was managed by Gene Mauch and went down in infamy months later. After building what seemed to be an insurmountable lead to capture the National League pennant, in the closing days of September the Phillies collapsed, dropping into a losing streak that enabled the St. Louis Cardinals to catch them from behind and advance to the World Series. Some people say Mauch never got over that, that he was haunted by losing that pennant until the day he died decades later.

Rookies could not bring their cars to spring training, so we had to walk everywhere if we couldn't get a ride from a veteran. One day, about five of us stopped at this restaurant. There were three white players, Pat Corrales, who had a Latin heritage, and me. The waitress came over and said, "Sir, I can't serve you." It hit me like a ton of bricks. This felt different than being in some rural town in Florida in the minors. I just said, "Hey, guys, I'll see you back at the hotel."

Corrales was a lighter-skinned Latino, with dark black hair in a brush cut, but two minutes after I walked out of the hotel, here he came, too. The manager told him he had to leave. I went to the Trailways bus station to eat. I didn't let the incident bother me too much at the time. That was the way it was done. From then on, the black players went to a restaurant called the Rosewood in the black area of town.

The Rosewood was only five or six blocks away from the ballpark. We met there and made friends with the local people. They all knew we were ballplayers there just for spring training. The only thing they didn't want was for us to mess with their girls. It was "lock up the daughters."

I never saw racial problems in Chatham, but the Phillies seemed to only have teams located in places sprinkled around the American South where racial issues were close at hand. I tried not to let the encounters bug me too much. I definitely didn't want them to hinder my advancement in the organization. As Martin Luther King Jr. said, I always kept my eyes on the prize. I figured I could put up with these inconveniences if I treated them only as inconveniences and didn't let them poison my attitude or distract me from my business.

It was ironic that I had to go to places like Nicaragua and Puerto Rico to be more fully welcomed, even though I didn't speak any Spanish at first. I was a stranger in those places, too, and I was there for the same reason, just to pitch and get better, but the people in the Latin American countries treated me as an equal.

In spring training, the main fun activity the black players indulged in was playing basketball. Alex Johnson, Grant Jackson, Johnny Briggs, and I always played. I was a good player, but not the best. I had always thought of myself as a pretty good basketball player, but the Americans were good. White players joined us. I didn't do anything fantastic. I was constantly reminded not to get hurt playing basketball. I was there for baseball. I didn't want to sprain an ankle or jam a finger.

Mauch was a tough manager and he didn't glad-hand the rookies. To him, I was just one of many prospects for the future. He watched me pitch, but didn't have much of anything to say. That season, Mauch was focused on the here and now because he felt he had the ingredients to win the World Series.

Pitching coach Al Widmar supervised my workouts, and I stuck with the major-league team until the last cut. I had not expected to make the team, so I was not terribly disappointed. Widmar's final words to me that spring were very encouraging. "Jenkins," Widmar said, "all you need is to get some experience and to work on your breaking pitches. Stick to it, and you'll be back with us."

In some ways I had made more of an impression with my bat than my arm. Nobody pays much attention to a pitcher's hitting, but I happened to be on a hot streak. One guy who noticed was Cal McLish, who was nearing the end of his 15-year, major-league pitching career. In fact, he appeared in just two games for the Phillies that season.

Calvin Coolidge Julius Caesar Tuskahoma "Buster" McLish became one of my best friends in baseball and played a huge role in my success in the big leagues. Cal had the longest name in the history of baseball, and he was not above teasing me. At the end of that spring training camp, McLish said, "You're a better hitter than you are a pitcher."

Cal won 92 games and lost 92 games in his major-league career. He had come up to the majors in 1944 when he was only 18. He knew a lot of baseball and turned out to be an even better teacher than player. Cal was still trying to hang on for one last year and wanted to be part of the pennant winner. But neither happened: the Phillies didn't win the pennant, and Cal didn't make it through the season in the majors.

But just as his stay in the majors was coming to an end, soon so was my time in the minors.

I started the 1964 season in Chattanooga, Tennessee, where the Phillies had a Double A team. In Chattanooga the manager was Frank Lucchesi again. It seemed as if we were on parallel journeys to the majors, moving up one classification at a time. He always talked to me about improving and working hard, about how that's what it would take for me to make it to the majors, and he gave me an opportunity to pitch.

There were a lot of pretty good pitchers in the Phillies' chain at the time. Guys like Dennis Bennett, Darold Knowles, and Rick Wise. But all of a sudden, I kind of leaped over them. I went 10-6 with a 3.11 earned-run average, made the Double A All-Star game in Birmingham, Alabama, and won a promotion back to Triple A Little Rock. That was my second stop in Little Rock.

Rick Wise, who had an 18-year major-league career with 188 wins, and I always seemed to end up together. A lot of times the Phillies would call you halfway through the season and move you up. The coach would say good-bye and tell you to "keep doing the right thing." It was apparent the Phillies were watching me and were interested in me.

It was probably a good thing I had not started my professional career in Little Rock. There was discrimination in Miami, and I learned to adjust to it, but things were tenser, more overt in Arkansas. Arkansas was one of the flashpoints of the civil rights movement. Orval Faubus was still the governor, and in 1957 he had become infamous for trying to defy laws that desegregated Arkansas schools. So it was not the most welcoming environment in the baseball world.

Richie Allen, Frank Barnes, Richard Quiroz, Marcelino Lopez, and I were the first black ballplayers for the Arkansas Travelers. We were segregated from the rest of the team and lived in a black area. We lived in a minister's house. Quiroz, a right-handed submarine pitcher, was from Panama. He was very light-skinned. We used to tease him, "Oh, you could pass for white." He didn't have much brown or tan color unless he got suntanned.

I think Richie's experiences in Little Rock changed him permanently. He grew up in Pennsylvania, and his first team in the minors was in Williamsport, Pennsylvania. He was a friendly and outgoing guy there. Later in his baseball career, Richie was portrayed as moody and divisive and hard to get along with. He was never hard to get along with until he felt the racism in Little Rock. In Little Rock, Richie was exposed to real racism for the first time, and it greatly stung him.

Richie had an old car with him, a 1953 Plymouth, and he gave the rest of us rides around town. One day, we came out of the ballpark and found the car covered with signs and scrawl on the windows. One message said, "We don't want you niggers—go home." Another said, "We never had any niggers before—you don't belong." Other signs on the car contained obscenities. We tore off the signs and drove home, but that was the beginning, and I think the insults affected Richie more deeply than they did the rest of us.

Of the five of us, Richie saw the most playing time. He was on the field every day and so took more verbal abuse than we did. When Richie misjudged a fly ball that landed over his head for a double, the home fans booed him. A few loudmouths used to ride him all the time. Richie was a great player, and he hit 33 home runs with 97 runs batted in, and that still didn't satisfy some of the fans. He hated it in Little Rock and said he dreamed of the day the Phillies got him out of there. "These country hicks are getting me down. I can't stand it," he said.

Richie took some solace in talking with his family long distance, but he told us he was going to quit the team and leave. "I don't have to take this abuse," he said. Richie was right. He should not have had to take that abuse. The Phillies talked him into staying in Little Rock for the rest of the season, but he began to hate the people there and got angry when sportswriters asked questions. Later on in Philadelphia, Richie got a reputation for being sullen and uncooperative, but he was always popular with teammates.

Away from the ballpark, we confined our activities to the black neighborhood. Each time we got a paycheck, we gave our host Reverend Rivers and his wife $50 apiece. She used it to buy groceries and cooked for us after the games. We didn't go out to eat at all. There weren't many places to go. The climate was one of big-time hostility to blacks.

The first time I was sent to Little Rock, in the first group of blacks to play for the Travelers, they still had signs in the locker room reading, "No black ballplayers on the team." There were segregated locker rooms, washrooms, and water fountains. The situation was kind of pressurized. We had our own black fans rooting for us who sat down the right-field line. The rest of the ballpark was the same, too, white-only washrooms, white-only water fountains, black-only washrooms, black-only water fountains.

There was always an undercurrent of racism in Little Rock. We were there to play ball, that's all. Richie suffered more than anyone else. Some of those bigoted fans were on him constantly. But he played hard. When Richie came to Little Rock, he didn't smoke. He started to smoke, as a nervous habit, I guess. He started to drink a little bit. It was the stress. The biggest influence in Richie's life was his mother. He complained to her about what was going on, but she told him to stick it out. Her advice was, "Do what you've got to do. You ain't going to be there long."

We were young guys, and a lot of times confronting that stress just got to be a little bit much. It was easy to think about going home. I try to be the kind of person who won't be distracted, who will persevere. I let a lot of the things that happened go right by me. It ate Richie up inside. I looked at it that being in Little Rock was a temporary situation and I could get through it and go on from there. I had ambition about going forward and becoming a member of the Philadelphia Phillies. I didn't want anything to stand in the way of that.

I finished the 1964 season 5-5 with the Arkansas Travelers and started the 1965 season in Little Rock, too, my third time on their roster. The Travelers used me as a relief pitcher a lot. It was my first taste of the bullpen and it was kind of training for how the organization thought of me. I didn't mind. I liked to think I had a rubber arm that could bounce back easily. I was a spot starter and a bullpen pitcher. In 1965 I finished 8-6 in Little Rock with a 2.95 earned-run average.

But my season wasn't over. At the end of the summer the Phillies called me up, and I became a big-leaguer. The team made me one of the end-of-season September call-ups. The Phillies also brought up Alex Johnson, Billy Sorrell, Grant Jackson, Pat Corrales, and Adolfo Phillips. We were in Little Rock, and after a game Frank Lucchesi gathered us together and said, "Boys, the Phillies want you. You have to be there tomorrow."

For the first year and a half or so in the minors, when I was in Miami and Chattanooga and Little Rock, Tony Lucadello continued to write me. It was nice. And he would telephone me in the winter. Once you were one of Tony's Boys, you were always one of Tony's boys. He didn't forget about you.

The big moment had come, not just for me, but for a group of us at the same time. You dream of how it will happen, what it will be like when you get the call to the majors, and it was terrifically exciting, but the reality also was that I hardly had any time to think. You never saw a group of guys pack so fast.

I had gotten married that spring to my first wife, Kathy. Kathy and I had met when we were young and attending church near Chatham. She was from Dresden, a short distance away, and from time to time the Baptist churches had meetings with different congregations and activities at community centers. I first noticed Kathy when there was a Sunday night roller-skating program. I was 17. She was a year and a half older. The skating alternated between men's choice and ladies' choice. We started skating together one night, and it became a regular weekly thing. I started asking her out on dates. After high school, Kathy enrolled in an all-girls Chatham school called the Pines Finishing School. She had been with me in Little Rock for a while, but went home to Chatham. I called her and had time to call my parents. I spoke to my father and told him I was going to the big leagues. He was very happy.

The six of us went to the airport together and flew off to join the Phillies. I moved into the bullpen. At the time, we didn't have a bullpen phone, so the coach had a system of hand signals. We each had our own hand sign, and if the bench waved, we began warming up.

The first time I warmed up, it probably only took me four or five pitches to get ready. Believe me, I was ready. The adrenaline was flowing. The day I got my first win, it took me no time to warm up. The Phillies were playing against the St. Louis Cardinals, at home in Connie Mack Stadium in Philadelphia on September 10, 1965. Bob Gibson was pitching for St. Louis. Jim Bunning, a future Hall of Famer and U.S. Senator from Kentucky, was our starting pitcher. He got into trouble, and they brought me into the game in the eighth.

Bunning's locker was located just a couple down from me, and I had picked his brains for pitching tips. I asked him how he gripped this type of pitch and how he did that. I just took it all in. And this was the pitcher I relieved in my major-league debut. I walked to the mound. Actually, I don't know if I walked to the mound. I don't remember if I walked or ran. I don't know how I got there. It could have been one of those *Star Trek* things where they say, "Beam me up, Scottie." I just got there.

Bunning was still there, the catcher was Pat Corrales, and manager Gene Mauch was there. Mauch gave me the ball and said, "Go get 'em, kid."

The first batter I faced was Dick Groat, the All-Star shortstop. The scouting report was that he was a first-ball, fastball hitter. I almost hit him with a pitch. He jumped out of the way, but the ball hit the bat. I struck him out on three pitches, a fastball and two sliders. The inning was over, and I went to the bench. I pitched more than four innings of relief, and we won the game 5–4 in 12 innings. It was the first victory of my major-league career. Pat Corrales doubled, went to third on a wild pitch, and scored on a single by Cookie Rojas.

A few weeks later, I pitched against the Mets and beat them. I got into seven games. Near the end of the season, I saw Wrigley Field for the first time when we played the Cubs. It was late September, and the Cubs were out of the pennant race, as they always were in those days. Wrigley was practically empty. Nobody was there. It was a dismal day. I got my first loss and the official attendance was 892. Can you imagine that?

My first impression of Wrigley Field was not a good one. No fans. No atmosphere. When I came on in relief, Ron Santo was at the plate, and he hit a high fly ball, home run, gone. The curious thing about the experience looking back decades later was that that was my only chance as a pitcher to beat the Cubs, and I didn't do it. Playing for the Cubs and in the American League during the course of my career, the Cubs and the Rangers were the only major-league teams I never beat.

A wind-blown home run was my first taste of Wrigley Field. Ron never teased me about the home run itself, but he did point out he was 1-for-1 against me lifetime.

That was a very interesting Phillies team to join. They had come so close to that pennant in 1964. It was crushing to lose a big lead in the standings and lose the pennant in the last few days of the season. It wasn't as if management gave up on that group, but the team officials wanted to infuse the roster with some young talent. There were veterans like Jim Bunning, who pitched two no-hitters, one of them a perfect game, and Chris Short, another very good pitcher, catcher Clay Dalrymple, outfielders Wes Covington and Johnny Callison, and infielder Tony Taylor, and the slugger Dick Stuart. But there were a lot of good, young players on the team, too. Rick Wise, Dennis Bennett, Ray Culp, and I were some of the young pitchers. Richie Allen was there. That team was also very heavy with black and Latin players. Just about half of the players on the 25-man roster were men of color.

Jim Bunning, the first player to win more than 100 games in each league, was very helpful to me. He wanted to win, and he would tell you anything you asked if he thought it would help the team. He was a hard-throwing pitcher, and he didn't worry about using his fastball to keep opposing batters off the plate. He let them know he was out there. And he won.

Professional athletes compete against one another for jobs all of the time, but they also forge bonds that last a lifetime. We were 18 to 21 years old when a lot of us first met, and although our careers took us on different paths, you could still make friends for life. Richie Allen and I are friends. I spent a lot of time with Rick Wise in the minors, and we were teammates with the Phillies and Red Sox. I still see Rick from time to time. He is a coach for a team in an independent league. Grant Jackson and I were roommates in minor league ball. Adolfo Phillips and I crossed paths more than once. Lee Elia and I played together in Buffalo, and he became a manager. Dallas Green was a player with me, and he became a manager.

One of the funny things that happened all of the time in the minors back then that you wouldn't see now is that everybody smoked. I didn't, but almost all my teammates did. You wouldn't catch athletes smoking now with all of the health information that has been brought out in the last 40 years. The old movies show ballplayers fooling around and giving each other a hot foot. One guy might distract a teammate while another guy came up behind him and light his shoes on fire. We really did that. Bobby Wine, the old Phillies shortstop, was good at it. Wes Covington was an oddball type of guy. Mostly guys did it while they were sitting on the bench.

A lot of guys chewed tobacco. When I was with the Texas Rangers, Sparky Lyle, the relief pitcher, used to pitch with a big chew in his cheek. He had an endorsement contract from Levi Garrett. Luis Tiant did that from time to time with the Red Sox. Once, when I was with the Rangers, I had my picture taken with a cheek full of bubble gum, and it came out on my baseball card. That was a one-time photograph.

Some of the hitters had quirky hitting styles. Wes Covington was a good hitter, but he held the bat practically sideways. For a while Richie Allen and Johnny Callison were using 40-ounce bats. They were like war clubs. Callison actually started that. They were strong guys. We called Chris Short, the pitcher, "Style." That's because he wanted every-thing to be just so. If he saw a rock on the mound, he would kick it off onto the grass. He only took one outfit on the road, a pair of pants, a sports coat, and a bunch of blue shirts and underwear. That's it. That was his style. He wore a slight variation of the same outfit every day.

We had a bunch of young guys who liked to have fun. Johnny Callison called me "Fudge" because I ate so many Fudgsicles. There was a cooler with Fudgsicles in it, and you could take what you wanted.

And then there was Bo Belinsky. He was a funny guy. Really funny. He pitched a no-hitter early in his career for the Angels, and he was the toast of the town in Los Angeles. He was a party animal. He had more chicks on the road than anyone I ever saw. You'd see him with different girls all of the time. There were always women hanging around the locker room and the hotel who wanted to meet him. He cultivated that image of being a playboy. Belinsky lived in Hawaii, but they called him "Hollywood" because he had been with the Angels and hung out with the movie stars. He dated Mamie Van Doren and other beautiful actresses.

Belinksy and Dean Chance, who was a better pitcher for the Angels, were like the movie stars of baseball for a while there. Chance had a better career and led the American League in earned-run average one season. I remember in an All-Star Game he was pitching, and Richie Allen came to the plate. Richie hit a home run off him that might not have landed yet.

The first time I saw Bo Belinsky, I thought he was Mexican. He had black hair, and his skin was so dark because of all the tanning he did. His other thing was never wearing underwear. He did work out hard and threw decently, but he didn't win too many games for the Phillies, and within a year he was gone. With Bo, you wondered if he woke up every morning to check and see if he was in the newspapers for something. Something besides baseball, I mean.

I had reached the majors in 1965 and was used in seven games during the season's final weeks. My record was 2–1 with a 2.19 earned-run average. My year had actually begun during my third season of winter ball again when I went back to Puerto Rico. I have no doubt that the time I spent during off-seasons learning in winter ball helped me get to the majors as quickly as I did.

There were a lot of really good players. Some, like Lou Johnson, had good major-league careers. Guys like Cleon Jones, Joe Foy, Jose Pagan, and Ellie Rodriguez were very good players who made the majors. A lot of the others would be the equivalent of Triple A hitters. I gained experience. A lot of those guys hit the ball hard. The lighting was decent in the parks. We played a lot of night games, and I know that you could get hit hard if you didn't know what you were doing. Many of the Mexican and Dominican players were there for the cash. It was not a vacation. I was there to learn something.

My second year in Puerto Rico, in Caguas, playing for Criollas—wouldn't you know it?—the manager was Frank Lucchesi. Someone might think Frank and I were Siamese twins—unless they looked at us closely, that is. Frank Lucchesi began grooming me for the position of long relief. He said the organization had nobody coming up who could do that job, and if I could, it would get me into the majors faster.

Also that winter, the pitching coach was Cal McLish. He taught me a slider. The emphasis was on keeping the ball low and being able to move the ball around on hitters. McLish stressed getting warmed up on about nine pitches in the pen and how to cope with every type of situation a reliever might face, from the number of outs to the number of base runners. For me, once I learned the slider, it opened up the door to what pitching was all about. I had a fastball, a curve, and a changeup. The slider was another weapon. That one extra pitch really put me in the big leagues. I knew I was doing something right when Roberto Clemente, Tony Perez, and Orlando Cepeda—all future Hall of Famers—couldn't pick it up in winter ball.

In that era a lot of guys had to work in the off-season anyway. This was my off-season job. But it was also my education. You had to have the right attitude to play winter ball. You had to realize you were going to a foreign environment and living in a different culture. Some guys went over and got into trouble.

The worst thing you could do was to find a girlfriend and get her pregnant. If you planned to leave and not take her with you, the entire city would be in an uproar. It was also easy for American players to go to a Latin country and have trouble with the umpires. If you bumped an umpire in winter ball, you got sent home fast. The game did not go in for skirmishes with the umpire. You could get in a fight with another player, but if you hit an umpire, you were gone. Guys that brought marijuana and got caught smoking it got sent home, too. I learned about the culture, and I learned some useful Spanish, how to order food and a cab.

I wanted to improve myself as much as I could. I led the Puerto Rican league in wins. Juan Pizarro, who was from Santurce, Puerto Rico, was second to me. He was a hero. Jose Pagan, the infielder with the Giants, was one of the top local players. When Kathy was over there with me, he invited us to a hometown barbecue. He was a super guy. I think what I did in Puerto Rico opened the doors for me, that the Phillies looked at me and said, "Hey, this young man could be ready for the big leagues." Cal McLish sent in good reports about me.

By the end of the 1965 season, I was convinced that I was in the big leagues to stay. All of the hard work running in the winter with Gene Dziadura, chopping wood, all of the encouragement Gene and Tony had given me, had paid off.

7

A Major Change

I had spent years thinking about playing for the Philadelphia Phillies and followed all of the workout plans and suggestions Gene and Tony gave me. Before I turned 23, I was in the majors with the Phillies.

A year later, in the spring of 1966, I was ready to assume a full-time role on the Phillies' pitching staff. However, in spring training I threw only about 20 innings. Part of me sensed that I was going to make the team and not be sent back to Triple A, but part of me wondered if the Phillies were going to make one last push for a pennant by relying mostly on a veteran pitching staff.

When the Phillies broke camp, I was with the big club. That was the good news. But mostly I sat around in a cleaned and pressed uniform, looking spiffy, but never getting sweaty. In the first couple of weeks of the season, I appeared in one game for the Phillies and threw two innings.

On April 21, 1966, I was out in the field during batting practice shagging fly balls before a night game when I was summoned to manager Gene Mauch's office by the bat boy. My first thought was that I was going to be sent back to Little Rock. Grant Jackson was out there with me, and I said, "Aw, man." I knew something was going to happen. When I got inside, I was surprised that John Quinn, the general manager, was there. Mauch told me to sit down and relax. John Herrnstein came in and sat down, but we were just hanging out there. Then, Adolfo Phillips came in. He was still wearing his street clothes.

It was not my imagination that the Phillies were committed to veteran pitchers. In fact, they wanted more of them. Phillips, Herrnstein, and I were swapped to the Cubs for Larry Jackson and Bob Buhl, two savvy veterans who fit the very description of what I had been thinking about. The young guys were expendable in the minds of the Phillies. Adolfo started to cry. Herrnstein had two kids and was trying to put down roots. I was newly married. And John Quinn goes, "Young men, you have 24 hours to report. You have 24 hours to be in Chicago." Mauch told us to get showered and changed, and in about 40 minutes the paperwork would be ready for us.

Mauch told us the Phillies were going for it that year and wanted to beef up for an immediate pennant run. He said specifically to me that I would fit in better with the Cubs because they were looking for young pitchers, and I was sure to get more of an opportunity in Chicago.

That was nice of Mauch to say, but what it meant was that I really didn't fit into the Phillies plans for later, either. After all of the time I spent with Gene and Tony, literally growing up with thoughts of making it with the Phillies, I was hurt that the organization gave up on me. I had never really had a passing thought of pitching for another team.

I was in a bit of a daze—and I know a lot of guys feel somewhat bitter and disappointed when they are traded for the first time—but I went back out on the field and said good-bye to some of the other players, especially ones I teamed with in the minors. It was like a kick in the stomach. I kind of had a bad taste in my mouth because I had expected to be a Phillie. I thought Philadelphia was where my future lay. I thought that with all of the things I had done to work with the Phillies over the years, going to those minor league places, pitching in winter ball, that maybe I didn't deserve a trade.

The other thought I had was that I had just been traded from a first-division National League club that was going to fight for the pennant to a bottom-division National League club that might finish last. In 1965 the Cubs finished in eighth place in a 10-team league with a record of 72–90. Then Leo Durocher came in as manager, made his famous statement about the 1966 club not being an eighth-place team, and got humiliated because the Cubs finished 59–103, placing 10th.

Kathy was in Philadelphia, staying at the Sheraton Hotel, when I called from the clubhouse. As soon as she heard my voice, she said,

"What's wrong?" I told her I had been traded to Chicago. Kathy's comment was, "Oh, no, Fergie, really?" And then she said, "Traded? You just came up!"

Kathy didn't have any problems with Chicago, but she was just expressing regret that the Phillies didn't want me. Although he was polite enough when informing me I was about to become Chicago property, Gene Mauch was later quoted in the newspapers saying that I "didn't throw hard enough, didn't have a big-league fastball." I never forgot that comment, and I used it for motivation over the years when I pitched against the Phillies. That worked out pretty well. Over the years, more than 70 percent of my decisions against the Phillies were victories.

I told Kathy to start packing and that we were going to leave right away. "We have to leave tonight?" she said. We did. We were going to drive. This was an era before computers and Mapquest. I told her to call the front desk and see if she could come up with a map.

When I hung up and went back through the locker room, Adolfo was still crying. Herrnstein was pissed off. He had just registered his kids for school. But I had to be concerned about getting myself to Chicago. Within an hour or so, Kathy and I had checked out of the hotel and were on the highway to Chicago. I had a brown Bonneville, a big car, and there was no traffic. We got into Chicago around 4:00 in the morning. It took us about eight hours. I remembered staying at a hotel called the Edgewater Beach or something the year before. It was pink. So we got a room there. The Cubs were scheduled to play the Dodgers at Wrigley Field. This was long before Wrigley had lights, and the Cubs played all home day games, so I wasn't going to get much sleep.

With everything that had been going on, I could hardly sleep anyway. I was kind of agitated. I set the alarm for 8:00 AM, and when it went off, I told my wife to go back to sleep and not come to the park. I got to Wrigley a little after 9:00 AM, and the first guy I met in the clubhouse was Ernie Banks, one of the greatest players in the game. The famous "Mr. Cub" said hello and congratulated me for being the newest member of the team. "Now you're a Chicago Cub," he said.

Yosh Kawano, the little clubhouse man who spent decades with the Cubs, came up to me and asked for all my sizes to get me a uniform that fit. I had had No. 30 with the Phillies, and I asked if I could have that number. He said in his broken English, "Mr. Jenkins, you can't have No. 30. Our number-one pitcher, Kenny Holtzman, has No. 30. But you can have No. 31." I said, "No problem, get me 31." I was born on the 13th of December, so I was just switching it around.

I went to the outfield and began shagging flies, right where I left off with Philadelphia the day before. Manager Leo Durocher came out and stopped to talk for a minute. He said he didn't know that much about me and asked what I thought my role would be with the ballclub. I said, "Well, the Phillies always groomed me to be a bullpen pitcher. I have a rubber arm so I can throw at least four days a week." I was still tall and a little bit skinny, and Durocher looked me up and down with some skepticism. "Yeah," I said, "I've got a strong arm. I might look thin, but I'm strong." He said okay. I was 6'5" and probably still only 180 pounds at the time. Eventually, I got my weight up to 210 pounds in the majors. I was tall, long-legged, with long arms.

I didn't really know Durocher back then. He was a dapper guy, with Hollywood pals. He wore $200 cashmere sweaters and $150 slacks and alligator shoes. He had suedes in all different colors. As a manager, he had a fearsome reputation as a tough guy who brooked no nonsense and could snarl at you. I wasn't afraid of him because I didn't know what guys thought of him when he managed the Dodgers and the Giants. I knew he won a lot. He was the boss and the guy I had to impress.

To start with, Durocher put me in the bullpen. We were playing the Dodgers, and Sandy Koufax just kicked the snot out of us. Koufax beat Dick Ellsworth in my first game with the team. The second game, Don Sutton was starting for Los Angeles, and we had Bob Hendley going. Bob was a good pitcher for the Cubs, but this day all of a sudden he lost it. It was only the third inning, and he had given up five hits and four walks. He couldn't throw strikes.

I was warming up. The pitching coach came out, and it was old Freddie Fitzsimmons. Fitzsimmons broke into the majors with the New

York Giants in 1925. This was 1966. He was old. Fitzsimmons talked to Hendley a little bit, walked around, and then went back to the dugout. Durocher came out and waved to the bullpen. I came in to face the shortstop John Kennedy. Two pitches later, he popped it up, and I was out of the inning. I pitched 5⅓ innings and got the win that day. I got off to a good start in Chicago. Not only did Durocher like the way I pitched that day, but one of the sportswriters in town, who covered the game for the *Chicago Tribune* actually wrote, "A star was born at Wrigley Field Saturday." I'm glad he had a crystal ball that could tell him that.

My only memory of Wrigley Field before that day was getting lit up for the home run by Ron Santo the previous September with fewer than 900 people in the park. Now it was April, the ivy wasn't even up on the walls. The fans had no expectations. But I was in the majors, and I had just won a game. I was feeling pretty good.

Although that year was terrible, the Cubs were building. We had some great ballplayers. There was Ernie Banks and Billy Williams, another Hall of Famer, who became a very good friend of mine. George Altman was a good hitter in the outfield, and the Cubs added infielders like Glenn Beckert and Don Kessinger and catcher Randy Hundley.

The Cubs had a very seasoned, knowledgeable coaching staff. Durocher was the leader, but he surrounded himself with good people like Peanuts Lowrey, Pete Reiser, Whitey Lockman, and Fitzsimmons. That was a lot of baseball experience on one bench. When we had meetings, and most of us were young, they imparted a lot of knowledge about the game. And Leo had been in the game for 40 years.

Durocher could be intimidating. That was just part of his personality. He really wanted to win, and he could come on very strong, even be mean, if he thought it was going to light a fire under a guy and help the team to win. It was definitely Durocher's way or the highway. He had an expression that he used all of the time, that if the current ballplayers weren't doing well, "I'll back the truck up." By that he meant he would ship out everybody and get other players who could win. He had that famous saying, "Nice guys finish last." What he said to us was, "There's nothing nice about baseball."

When Durocher called a clubhouse meeting, we either stood around the edge leaning against pillars or we sat on stools. We always faced the middle of the room, and he paced back and forth there, lecturing us, yelling at us. He ridiculed some guys by name, right to their faces and in front of everyone else. Durocher was bald, had piercing blue eyes, and a gruff voice. For such a hard-nosed guy, it was strange that he played cards with the players in the locker room. He didn't seem like a buddy-buddy manager, but if Leo played gin rummy with you, then you knew you were on his good side. Ken Holtzman, the terrific left-handed pitcher who threw two no-hitters for the Cubs, was a favorite card-playing partner of Durocher's.

In those days, it was assumed that starting pitchers were also finishing pitchers, that when the manager gave you the ball you were going to complete the game, unless you got hurt or shelled. Eventually, the close relationship between Holtzman and Durocher deteriorated. Durocher started calling Holtzman's pitches from the bench, and Holtzman pitched worse. Durocher started yanking Holtzman in the seventh inning, and a frustrated Holtzman just felt he couldn't communicate with Durocher anymore.

Durocher was very hard on Ernie Banks. He was unfair, really, to him. Ernie had been there for years, had been an All-Star, and he was Mr. Wrigley's favorite. Leo resented that. He got it in his head that Ernie was too old and couldn't produce. Four different times in the late 1960s, Durocher tried to give away Ernie's first-base job, and each time Ernie won it back because he produced better than any of the substitutes.

Leo gave the first base job to Lee Thomas. There was a rookie named John Boccabella. He tried Willie Smith. He gave it away, and Ernie won it back. He hit 20 home runs, or he hit 30 home runs. He just won the job back each time. One thing that drove Durocher nuts was that, at that point in Ernie's career, when he was 35 or 36 years old, you didn't have to be Einstein to know he wasn't going to steal any bases. So Ernie took tiny leads off first base, like three inches. He wasn't going to steal, and he sure as heck wasn't going to let himself get picked off. Durocher screamed to the first-base coach, "Get him off! Get him off!" Meaning he wanted him to make Ernie take a bigger lead so if someone got a hit he might make it to third base safely.

That went on the whole year. The rest of us, sitting on the bench, watching and listening, just wanted to turn to Leo and say, "Give it a rest!" But nobody did that. Ernie was just the greatest guy. He was a lot of fun to be with. He always talked when he was in the field. He was always bubbly and great to be around. Durocher seemed to be the only person on planet Earth who had trouble getting along with Ernie Banks.

Leo found fault with everybody, me included. That was his thing. Pitching to certain hitters, I might throw the wrong pitch, and Durocher said, "You've been in the big leagues less than two years and won some games, but you're not there yet." He needled guys. He wanted them to use his words as motivation, but I don't think he could help himself, anyway. That was just his personality. Once I started winning 20 games in a season, however, he let me call my own ballgame.

Once I became an established starting pitcher, Durocher seemed to gain more respect for me. Over time, he gained more confidence in me and catcher Randy Hundley working together to call the game.

One thing I enjoyed the most about being on that Cubs team in 1966 was being a teammate of Robin Roberts. He was in his final season in the majors, and he was my idol. He was a great pitcher and a great guy. He was just finishing his career, and I was just starting mine, but we ended up with almost the exact same number of victories. I had 284 and Robin Roberts had 286. He got his last two wins with the Cubs that season.

I was the Cubs' long relief man in 1966. I pitched in 60 ballgames, finished 6–8, and had an earned-run average of 3.31. A lot of people warned me about Durocher's temper and temperament. I heard so much bad stuff that when I got traded to the Cubs I thought I was going to play for the Devil. It turned out that after I met the Devil, I kind of liked him.

My role began changing with the Cubs when Leo told me he was going to start me on May 21 against the Atlanta Braves. For a guy who made his living the rest of his career as a starter, I gave an answer few people would predict. I said, "Why me? I like the bullpen." Durocher said he was short of starters. In my first big-league start, I went five and a third innings and left the game with a 4–3 lead.

Eight days later, Durocher started me again against the Braves. I went 8⅓ innings, struck out 10, and we won 3–2 in extra innings. The boss told the press, "We've found another starting pitcher. Fergie's beautiful."

The Cubs were young and by most statistical measures inept that summer, but we were playing for the future. Durocher saw talent in the youngsters and knew we would get better. He felt his task was to instill more confidence in us and shape us into tougher, more consistent ballplayers.

By the end of the season, I had started 12 games, and the Cubs won eight of them. Also by the end of that season, Durocher had decided that I would become a full-time starting pitcher. The Cubs sent me to the Arizona Instructional League in Scottsdale for a month after the season to work on my pick-off move, holding runners on base, and pitching more from a stretch, all things I would need to use more often as a starter. The 1966 season was the turning point of my career.

When I got back to Chatham, I was given nice treatment by the hometown folks. The *Chatham Daily News* featured a two-page spread on me and my exploits. The banner headline read, "Welcome Home, Fergie!" In other parts of the section were such messages from local businesses reading, "Well Done, Fergie" and things like that. Chatham Mayor Garnet Newkirk declared October 21 to be Ferguson Jenkins Day. Someone made up a Fergie sweatshirt and sold them with the proceeds going to charity. There was a parade and a big banquet.

I always knew Chatham was proud of me, but those events recognizing my breaking through in the majors were pretty special.

8

Starting for the Cubs

It was the right time to join the Chicago Cubs. The Cubs had been an afterthought in the National League pennant race for years. Ernie Banks would predict a pennant every year in spring training. Sometimes Ernie's predictions would rhyme. But he was the only one who ever predicted the Cubs would win, and he was wrong every year.

The Cubs held spring training in Scottsdale, Arizona, and I had it in my head that I was going to come in from Canada and win a spot in the starting rotation. We had 17 or 18 pitchers on the 40-man roster, so things were wide open. Durocher worked us hard. It was a daily grind. He wanted us in the best shape we could possibly be in. I didn't take anything for granted. I threw a lot of batting practice. I did a lot of running. In all of the workouts and all of the drills, I told myself never to be last. Be the first in line to run, be ready to throw BP. I took that attitude all of the time. If you want to do things, you've got to get noticed first. Be right there. I tried to let people know I was present and accounted for.

I pitched some good games in spring training against San Francisco and the Angels. I think that's why Leo gave me the opportunity to be the Opening Day starter in 1967.

Things began to change for the Cubs under Durocher. We were awful my first year in Chicago, but when I came back in 1967 in the rotation, it didn't take long before I realized I had found my niche. All of my workouts and time spent in winter ball combined to develop me into a once-every-four-days, major-league starting pitcher. It was as if I had been transformed overnight, only it had hardly been overnight. It had taken me years to reach this spot.

My first season as a starting pitcher I finished with a 20–13 record and was selected for the league All-Star team. I had 20 complete games. I don't know if that classifies as having a rubber arm, but in modern-day baseball, they would build a statue to honor a Cubs pitcher who completed 20 games. Times and methods have changed. I also struck out 236 batters that season. That broke the team record of 205, set by Orval Overall in 1909. I finished second in the Cy Young Award voting for selection as the best pitcher in the league.

Pitching coach Joe Becker kept his eye on my form and delivery, and always gave me instruction and encouragement. Once he saw the success I was having as a starter, Joe told me to forget about becoming a reliever ever again and make sure I built up my stamina so I never missed my turn in the rotation.

"You can't make any money pitching once a week," he said. "If you want me to make you a millionaire, you've got to go out there every fourth day. If you do that, you'll get 40 starts. Win half of those, and you'll be a 20-game winner."

Joe's numbers were almost exactly on the money, so to speak. I won 20 out of 38 starts.

I was lined up to pitch Opening Day against the Phillies. On the days when I took my pitching turns, I was not as friendly and open to chitchat as usual. I tried not to be too grumpy, but I was focused and serious. I was caught off guard that day when I heard my name called from the stands and looked up to see my parents. I was pretty surprised. I had just enough time to run over and hold my mother's hand and shake hands with my dad. But I didn't have time to socialize.

At different points in the game, I heard my mom yelling, "C'mon, baby! C'mon, Fergie!" I won the game, but my concentration wasn't as sharp as it should have been. Chatham's mayor, Archie Stirling, sent me a telegram of congratulations afterward. As always, Chatham kept its eyes on me. In my game with the Cubs, I hit a home run. I was always a pretty good hitting pitcher. I hit six home runs in one season in Chicago, and I held the team record for a pitcher for more than 40 years until Carlos Zambrano tied it.

After that, I made it a point to invite my parents in advance when I thought I was going to pitch Opening Day. Not only was I chosen for the All-Star team that summer, but I got into the game. It was played in Anaheim. I came in to relieve Juan Marichal. One highlight was striking out Mickey Mantle. National League manager Walt Alston thought I might be nervous pitching to Mantle and came out to talk to me before the Yankee star's at-bat. I had pitched half of a season as a starter, and I had faced the best hitters in the National League, so I was not particularly nervous. He said, "You know who's hitting?" I said, "Of course." And he said, "Go get him." I knew Mantle was a great hitter. It was exciting striking him out, though. I think the catcher was Joe Torre. I had five more strikeouts in three innings, but I gave up a home run to Brooks Robinson. The game lasted 15 innings.

There were a bunch of galas leading up to the game, and everyone in baseball was there. We had a dinner, and they presented us with All-Star rings. It was a pretty special occasion to represent your ballclub for the National League. Warren Giles was president of the National League, and he came into the locker room to give us a little pep talk. He said, "We are the team. We are the senior team." He made it clear that he wanted us to carry ourselves seriously and try to win.

The most frustrating thing about 1968 was losing five games by 1–0 scores. That meant I was pitching terrifically, but on those occasions the Cubs didn't score runs. That was an era of top-notch pitching. There were a lot of low-scoring games. After the 1968 season, when Bob Gibson recorded an earned-run average of 1.12 and Denny McLain won 31 games, baseball officials felt the game had become imbalanced, with the rules favoring pitchers too much. You probably wouldn't get a pitcher to admit such a thing, but the leagues lowered the mounds, and batting averages did go up again.

At the beginning of the 1967 season, I decided to save a game ball from each win. Clubhouse manager Yosh Kawano helped me out. After each victory, Yosh wrote the line score and the name of the opposing pitcher on each ball. I put the balls in a shoebox and kept it in my locker. I had a pretty nice souvenir collection at the end of the season. Twenty wins is a milestone, the magic number for pitchers. I kept up the habit of saving the balls from wins for three seasons. But since I won more than 20 games each year, I started to gather too many baseballs, so I stopped the practice. In the years after that, I just saved the ball from my last win of the year.

It was a good start for me, but there was still plenty of room to improve and become a better all-around pitcher. I finished 15-5 at Wrigley Field. Now that's a nice home-field advantage. But my road record was 5-8. If Wrigley was the Friendly Confines for me, as it is often called, I needed to make other ballparks into my friend, too.

One sign of a pitcher's maturity is the attitude he brings to the mound. When I first started pitching in high school, I was a thrower. I didn't plan my pitches. I didn't think about how I would make a batter hit the ball in a certain direction. All I wanted to do was blow the ball past him and dazzle him with my fastball. You always get a little charge when that happens, but when you are a major-league pitcher, you can't dwell on that play. There's always another batter ready to step in and take you deep, even if you just made the last one look foolish with a blistering pitch that froze him.

You learn you should be patient, that you should throw your next pitch when you are ready. You are in command. The ball is in your hand. Nothing is going to happen on that field until you throw the ball. Don't be in too much of a hurry. They say Dizzy Dean once stepped off the rubber, turned his back to the plate, and watched an airplane fly overhead for a few long seconds. It was his little personal time out. Spectators were looking at the sky. When Dean was ready, he went back to the business of pitching. You can't take all day because the umpire will come out and ask what the heck you are doing, but you have time to compose yourself and think about what you're going to throw.

The day before I was scheduled to take my pitching turn, I was the designated Cub in the dugout charting pitches. That was a mental exercise, to refresh your memory of what their left- or right-handed batters liked to hit. It gave us a chance to study a player if he was new in the lineup. A lot of times I would walk past the batting cage when the visiting team was hitting and watch their guys take batting practice. The extra men hit first, so if you saw someone you thought was starting to hit with the extra men, it meant they might have a nagging injury and might not play or might have a problem in the batter's box. Very seldom did the regulars hit with the extras back then. It was taboo.

If the pitcher for us was Kenny Holtzman, a southpaw, pitching the day before me against the team, I might not gain as much from charting pitches as if Bill Hands, another right-hander, was pitching. The hitters might react differently when the ball was coming from the other side from Holtzman.

Pittsburgh was a team that had a lot of good hitting right-handed swingers. They just had a good batting order. Matty Alou, Gene Alley, Roberto Clemente, Willie Stargell, Bill Mazeroski. I had to be stingy with my runs. The Cardinals, from time to time, and the Phillies, had good hitting lineups. There were only 10 teams in the league at the time, and every team had some hard hitters.

Certain pitchers match up well against certain hitters, regardless of reputation or statistics. I think I gave up two home runs to Hank Aaron in 11 years. I got Willie Mays out pretty regularly. The reverse of that was trying to get Hall of Famers Willie "Stretch" McCovey or Orlando Cepeda out. You knew McCovey wasn't going to take the day off when he played against me.

I would get one of those big sluggers out one inning and kind of go, "Whew!" and then there they would be, waiting to hit against me again. They came around so fast, it was as if they got two turns in the batting order. There was big Willie McCovey, down on one knee in the on-deck circle, waving two bats as if they were toothpicks, going, "Yeah, okay, my turn is next." There were guys like Pete Rose, the Hit King, who you knew were just going to get their hits. They might go 0-for-4, but the next game they would get you.

When I played with the Cubs, there was a different atmosphere between teams at the ballpark. You might have become friends with other players on the way up through the minors, being former teammates, playing in All-Star Games, or playing together in winter ball, but there was strictly no fraternization at the batting cage or on the field before the game. That rule was enforced, not like today where guys on different teams hug each other before the game. When he came to town, I ate dinner with Alex Johnson. I ate dinner with Grant Jackson, and Tito Fuentes, whenever I saw him. Sometimes when they came to Chicago, I invited them over to the house. We would go to a local bar for drinks. We were friends, but not at the ballpark.

Off the field, if they knew I was going to pitch, they would laughingly say, "Take it easy on me tomorrow, Jenks." I would say, "I'm not going to take it easy on you. And you're not going to take it easy on me." Sooner or later, it seemed, everyone got traded or changed teams. Nowadays, I often see Tom Seaver. I see Steve Carlton in Colorado. I see a lot of the big-name players from that era now when I go places, and we talk. There's a big-time respect there.

Tom Seaver told me he named a Labrador retriever after me in the 1960s, called it Fergie. When I was still playing, and I talked to other guys away from the park, they told me about the best places to fish in their areas. They knew that was one of my hobbies, so they tipped me off.

I first met Reggie Jackson when he was about 21 years old with the Oakland Athletics in spring training in Arizona. There were only a few teams training in Arizona back then. I invited him to dinner. Reggie was a thin player at the time, not bulked up. He started bulking up with Baltimore and got bigger when he was with the Yankees. There was probably a little more familiarity between the guys who trained in Arizona because there were fewer teams than in Florida. We played against each other so often. You tried to figure out their strengths and weaknesses, so if you saw them during the regular season, you would know their habits. You knew them, and they knew you, too.

In 1967 the Cubs' record was 87–74, good for third place in the National League. We were a young and talented club on the rise. Randy Hundley was the catcher. Ernie was still there at first. Ron Santo held down third, Glenn Beckert was set at second base. Billy Williams was a mainstay in left field. And our pitching was good. Kenny Holtzman, Bill Hands, Ray Culp, and Joe Niekro were on the team.

Fergie, age 9 months, with his mother, Delores Jenkins. PHOTO COURTESY OF FERGIE JENKINS

Fergie's father, Ferguson Sr., played on the 1938–1939 Chatham All-Star baseball team in Chatham, Ontario. PHOTO COURTESY OF FERGIE JENKINS

Fergie played for the Harlem Globetrotters in 1967 and 1968. He is shown standing, second from right, in this team photo signed by Curly Neal (lower left). PHOTO COURTESY OF FERGIE JENKINS

Fergie gets a kiss from his mom at Wrigley Field in April 1967. She and Ferguson Sr. (right) had traveled to Chicago to watch their son pitch courtesy of Ernie Miller (in back), sports editor of the London (Ontario) Free Press. PHOTO COURTESY OF AP IMAGES

A young and determined Fergie at the Cubs' Arizona training camp in 1967. PHOTO COURTESY OF AP IMAGES

Fergie pitching against the Mets–the team that would eventually catch the Cubs in the pennant race–in July 1969. PHOTO COURTESY OF AP IMAGES

Fergie is joined at the Cubs' training camp in Scottsdale, Arizona, by Ferguson Sr. and a friend of his father's. PHOTO COURTESY OF FERGIE JENKINS

Fergie on the mound for the Texas Rangers at The Ballpark in Arlington. Fergie had two stints in Texas, pitching for the Rangers in 1974–75 and 1978–81. PHOTO COURTESY OF GETTY IMAGES

Fergie's last major-league season was with the Cubs in 1983. Here he confers with Jody Davis on the mound during an early contest from that year. PHOTO COURTESY OF GETTY IMAGES

Fergie in action with the Red Sox versus the Indians in Cleveland on July 13, 1977. He pitched for Boston during the '76 and '77 seasons. PHOTO COURTESY OF GETTY IMAGES

Fergie pitched for the Winter Haven Super Sox of the short-lived Senior Professional Baseball Association in 1989. PHOTO COURTESY OF FERGIE JENKINS

Fergie celebrates Christmas with his family at Disney World in Orlando, Florida. PHOTO COURTESY OF FERGIE JENKINS

In 2004, Fergie received an honorary Doctor of Laws degree from McMaster University in Hamilton, Ontario. PHOTO COURTESY OF FERGIE JENKINS

Fergie—the only Canadian honored at Cooperstown—waves to the crowd after the playing of "Oh Canada" during his induction into The National Baseball Hall of Fame on July 25, 2004. PHOTO COURTESY OF AP IMAGES

Fergie with his wife, Lydia, and grandson, Kaleb—a budding athlete in his own right. PHOTO COURTESY OF FERGIE JENKINS

Fergie took over as the Cubs pitching coach in 1995. Here he keeps a close eye on Jaime Navarro, warming up during spring training of that season. PHOTO COURTESY OF GETTY IMAGES

One funny thing was that Curt Simmons was on the team, the same Curt Simmons I had seen so many years earlier on the cover of the sports magazine wearing a Phillies uniform. Simmons was at the tail end of his two-decades-long career. He went 3-7 with the Cubs and completed his major-league stay with the Angels that very season. It was kind of amazing that I did get to wear that same Philadelphia uniform that had inspired me as a kid. I remember running my hand across the front and feeling the raised letters. They were embroidered on. That was a brief thrill. But I was no longer a member of the Phillies' organization. I was a Cub.

I took to heart the advice Gene Dziadura gave me about keeping my pitching arm covered at all times—Wrigley Field was a place where it was good to practice that procedure. I always wore a long-sleeved shirt, but I also always wore a team jacket on the bench. I took warm showers. I put heat on my arm. I never iced it. Part of it was psychological, but I think keeping my right arm warm made it readier to throw. It just kept my body warm and kept me in game mode. After games, I wrapped a towel around my arm and stood in a hot shower and let the water run down on it.

At Wrigley, there always seemed to be wind. That would have cooled my arm off. The wind is a factor in so many games at Wrigley. In April and in parts of May, the wind blows in. As it gets warmer over the summer, the wind blows out and across. It becomes more of a hitter's park.

I developed a strategy to cope with the wind. With the wind blowing out, the ball is going to fly. I tried to run the ball in on hitters' hands, trying to jam them. In Chicago, driving to the park, I could look inside and see which way the wind was blowing, or not blowing. Then I knew what I had to do. The ballpark was a little less friendly when the wind was blowing, but when the vines grew, the grass was plush, and fans were jumping around in the bleachers, Wrigley became more friendly. I enjoyed pitching there.

The home ballpark is a park where you ought to win more than on the road. I used to connect with the fans in a lot of ways. When I finished warming up for the game and I walked down the foul line to the dugout, I used to give away a couple of the balls. Kids yelled, "Can I have one?" And I said, "No problem." The bullpen mounds at Wrigley are right in front of the stands and the dugout.

I spent a long time warming up. I went to the bullpen mound about half an hour or so before the start of the game. I threw 100 pitches every time. Joe Becker counted them. Other pitchers probably throw 45 or 50. I always wanted to be ready in the first inning. It was my theory that more runs are scored in the first three innings of games, so if you could shut out the opponent for the first three innings, it made for a little easier game. I never wanted to give up runs early because that meant the team had to battle back.

Fans at home and on the road always talked to me while I was warming up. They told me how tough my opponent was if it was Bob Gibson or Tom Seaver, or they said that Ernie Banks would have to hit a bunch of home runs for me to win. I heard them. Being the number-one pitcher in the rotation meant I faced guys like Gibson, Seaver, Carlton, and Marichal a lot. To me, that was part of what it was all about.

My first impression of Wrigley Field and the Cubs was quite negative the year before, but when I became a Cub, that changed quickly enough. I found out that the sun did shine some of the time. I discovered that Wrigley Field was a beautiful ballpark when the ivy grew in. There were only 892 fans in the ballpark the day I surrendered that home run to Ron Santo, but in 1967 we attracted nearly one million fans. We gave the baseball fans of Chicago a winning team.

Chicago was a fresh start for me. Chicago was also a fresh start for Leo Durocher. And 1967 was also a fresh start for the Cubs.

9

Winning in Chicago

The players came out of the 1967 season believing the organization was putting together a Cubs team that could contend for a pennant. We improved to 13 games over .500 in 1967 after being 44 games under .500 the year before. We were not the National League doormat anymore.

As a player on a team that makes a turnaround like that, you are pretty proud. It means the hard work paid off. You have sense of accomplishment, and you have a sense that you are part of something that is growing and improving.

I won my 20th game at the very end of the season. I won it, and two days later I was driving back to Canada. There was no champagne in the clubhouse. Everybody shook hands and everybody was pretty happy about what we had done that season. The way the season unfolded, with my doing a good job as a starter, I acquired the goal of winning 20 games. Every pitcher wants to do that. It is something permanent, something that stays with you when people talk about your career and ask what you accomplished. I can say, "I was a 20-game winner in the big leagues." I liked the sound of that. It gave me a secure feeling. I had no way of knowing that that was going to be the first of six straight seasons of winning at least 20 games with the Cubs.

The Cubs came out of the 1967 season with a good attitude. We had a feeling of "What's next?" I told myself to go home, get some rest, and come back with the same type of confidence I had developed. Gene Dziadura put together a workout schedule for me that I followed starting right after Christmas. It felt good knowing we were a better club in 1967 than we had been in 1966, and I felt we would be even better in 1968.

Joe Becker said winning a lot of games would make me a million-dollar pitcher, but I was a long way from that tax bracket after my first 20-game season. I was making $6,500 a year when I came over from the Phillies. The Cubs doubled my salary to $13,000 after my season of long relief. That was a big raise since a lot of times teams only handed out $500 raises. I figured after winning 20 games they should double my salary again. They didn't do that, but I did get a $10,000 raise.

I needed a bigger income because I was married and was starting to raise a family. My wife, Kathy, was with me when I started out with the Phillies, and she was with me when I got traded to Chicago. It made for a hectic lifestyle. We were young and in love, and it didn't seem that big a deal to move around at first.

Kathy and I had three daughters: Kelly, whom we adopted in 1969; Delores, who was named after my mother and whom Kathy gave birth to in 1970; and Kimberly, who was born six years later. Kathy was with me throughout my entire major-league baseball career, but in 1984, after I retired, it did not seem as if we were getting along very well. We moved toward a divorce, though it didn't become final until 1986.

I was very pleased to become a 20-game winner in 1967, but if someone had told me that I was going to put up six 20-game seasons in a row, one of the best stretches of pitching in baseball history, I would have said they were dreaming. But Joe Becker was right. If I stayed healthy and got my 40 starts, I would win 20 games.

The way teams used pitchers and the attitude of pitchers was totally different 40 years ago than it is today. If you look at my statistics, you see that I threw 289⅓ innings in 1967, 308 in 1968, 311⅓ in 1969, 313 in 1970, 325 in 1971, 289⅓ in 1972, and 271 in 1973, all with the Cubs. In only one of those seasons, 1971, did I lead the National League in innings pitched. Pitchers are lucky to reach 225 innings now. The vast majority of pitchers throw fewer than 200 innings. It's the age of specialization, with a closer to end the game, a setup man in the eighth inning, a middle reliever, a long reliever. They call pitching six innings and giving up three runs or less a "quality start." Well, that's a 4.50 earned-run average. If a starting pitcher had a record like that when I was pitching, he would have been either benched or sent back to the minors. We were work horses, and we were expected to be work horses. Now complete games have become a rarity, never mind throwing 20 of them in a season.

I could handle that type of workload. I'm sure part of it was good genetics and my rubber arm. I could bounce back after three days off. I enjoyed it. No problem. It was my goal to pitch a shutout and go nine innings every time I started a game. Of course, I hoped my teammates would score some runs for me, too. During the 1968 season, I lost games nine times where the Cubs got shut out. My record was 20-15, but I should have won 30 games that year. I know Bob Gibson got me 1-0 in that season where he hardly gave up any runs all year. I ran into Don Drysdale when he was in the middle of setting the record for throwing the most innings without allowing a run. I ran into other pitchers when they were hot, too. That was the year of the pitcher.

Actually I was quite lucky I got to pitch at all during the 1968 season. While we were in spring training in Arizona, I had a horse-riding accident that could have ruined the rest of my career. Ron Santo suggested that when we got some free time between workouts or games we should combine a day of playing golf and riding horses. It sounded like fun.

When we got to the riding stable, the workers gave me an old mare to ride that looked as if it were about to give birth. I was with a small group that rode a little bit ahead on the trail out into the desert. We decided to wait for Joe Niekro and Rich Nye to catch up. But when I turned around to look for them, my horse decided to put down the hammer and race back to the stable. My efforts to slow her down were like hitting broken brakes in a car. She never stopped until she ran right into Nye and his horse. I was not riding this horse, this horse was riding me. She kept on going back to the stable, and when I pulled on the reins for a right turn, she chose to go left. I was catapulted out of the saddle, crashed into a wire fence, and landed on the ground with a loud thump.

I not only looked as if I had been in a wreck, I was a wreck. My blue jeans were torn. My face was bruised. One leg had a bloody gash. And my right arm, my pitching arm, had a bad scratch. My teammates surveyed the damage and took me to the hospital. They were more scared than I was that one of their meal tickets was going to miss considerable playing time. I was treated and released, but I didn't try to hide the damage from Leo Durocher. I called him right away. Perhaps I was hoping he might say something like, "Fergie, I'm just glad you're all right." That's not quite the way it happened. He let loose with a string of profanity, using words I am still trying to find in the dictionary or thesaurus. And he wasn't brief. He went on for the equivalent of a printed page.

That wasn't the end of the incident, either. General manager John Holland called me up and berated me for my foolish judgment. He wasn't as colorful as Durocher, but he let me know what he thought. "I thought you had more sense than that," Holland said of my ride. He basically suggested that this could cost the Cubs the pennant. Durocher did not compliment the other players who took horseback rides, either.

I am not sure if such an accident could be hidden from the press these days, though I do see how much pro football coaches try to hide injury information. But we put out the word to the media that I had a pulled muscle and that's why I could not work the last two weeks of spring training. I took a bruising. I couldn't walk for two days. My entire right side was swollen and discolored from my ankle to my pelvis. A blood clot developed in my leg.

The plan was for me to pitch the second game of the 1968 season. All day long I loaded up on painkillers. By the time the first pitch was scheduled, I couldn't feel a thing. I was numb. I won the game and struck out 12. I even hit one of our five home runs. I was still high at the end of the game. I want to say I floated to the clubhouse. However, when the painkillers wore off, I couldn't walk for two days.

I coped with discomfort for a long time, but I eventually got my pitching groove back. The aches and bruises suffered when I was thrown by the horse probably contributed to my 8-9 start by the All-

Star break. But I started 40 games again in 1968 and had a record of 20-15. My earned-run average was 2.63, the best of my career. When I came back for my second season as a full-time starter, I felt I had emerged as a baseball player, but I also felt there were still some skeptics who thought my previous year was a fluke. That was a good impetus to do it again.

There was a lot of tension on the Cubs early in the season, some of it black and white. Lou Johnson was a new member of the team. He was a solid hitter and all-around player, someone active in the civil rights movement and outspoken. There was no problem with that. But when Martin Luther King Jr. was assassinated on April 4, 1968, there was an unfortunate confrontation. Johnson and Billy Williams, both black, got into an elevator already occupied by Randy Hundley, who is white. Hundley said, "I heard your man got shot."

Johnson, whose emotions were already raw, erupted in a rage, and he and Hundley screamed at one another. Johnson shouted, "Stop this damned elevator. I'm not riding with you." The moment passed, but the feud did not. Opening Day in Cincinnati was postponed four days, until April 8. We were in Ohio to start the season, but there were riots in the streets in Chicago, the anger at King's assassination spilling over.

Johnson and Hundley avoided each other in the locker room, and gradually Johnson alienated other players. The chemistry of the locker room was shattered. In June Johnson was traded to the Cleveland Indians for Willie Smith. That didn't end the turmoil, though. Johnson gave a newspaper interview where he accused certain Cubs of being racists and blasted Durocher for playing favorites. I thought Johnson's tirade was a lot of sour grapes.

My old friend, Adolfo Phillips, traded with me from Philadelphia to Chicago, had trouble adjusting. He was injured frequently and didn't play well when healthy. Phillips lost it one day after getting hit by a pitch and shouted that Durocher was not "taking care" of him by instructing pitchers to throw at opposing hitters to protect the Chicago lineup. Ron Santo and Billy Williams calmed Adolfo down, but Durocher did urge the pitchers to be more aggressive with brushback pitches.

After all of that stuff, we rallied in the second half to finish with an 84-78 record. We were third in the league again. It was not what we had hoped for when the season began, but there were lessons to be learned about staying on the same page and pulling our talent together. We definitely thought we had a pennant run in us.

That was the summer that the Democratic National Convention took place in Chicago. It was a heated time in American society, with the Vietnam War firing up and the civil rights movement on everyone's minds. Kenny Holtzman was a member of the Illinois National Guard, and he was called up to serve in the middle of the season. He traded his Cubs cap for a hard helmet, and his Cubs uniform for a soldier's uniform as thousands of young people demonstrated in the streets. One minute Kenny was with us, the next he was down the street in a different arena.

By my second year with the Cubs, I also think I had the full sense of how big the rivalry was between the Cubs and the Cardinals. It had nothing to do with how the teams were doing in the standings and everything to do with Chicago and St. Louis being about 250 miles apart—and that they had been playing against each other for decades. Fans in Southern Illinois overlapped, too. The Cardinals always had a really top pitcher I had to go against, whether it was Bob Gibson, Steve Carlton, or Rick Wise.

A pretty funny thing happened in my early days with the Cubs. I had tried chewing tobacco and didn't like it, so I switched to bubble gum. That seemed to suit me, and I kept my gums moving during games. Once, rather absent-mindedly, I blew some bubbles, and it was noticed by the TV cameras. This did not play well in the Cubs organization. P.K. Wrigley, owner of the Cubs, was the patriarch of a business that made its mark and its money by selling gum. But not bubble gum, other brands like Juicy Fruit and Doublemint.

My gaffe was brought to the attention of Mr. Wrigley, who must have said something to Leo. The Jenkins error in judgment resulted in a tongue-lashing from Leo that was applied to the whole team. The rule was laid down. "At no time—never, never, never—will any of you chew bubble gum again," Durocher roared. "If I catch you chewing bubble gum again, I'll send you so far down into the minors that a 10-cent stamp won't reach you!"

I became a Doublemint man, and never again did I blow bubbles as large as a grapefruit. It was a lost art for me, but I think I made the wise choice in the context of my career.

I had heard Durocher equated with the Devil when I first became aware of him, but I think his other nickname, "Leo the Lip," was the most appropriate because Durocher would say anything and say it loudly. He was usually complimentary to me, though. It was always good to be on the good side of Leo Durocher. You did not want to be on his bad side. I didn't want to be in the "Hey, I'll back the truck up" category. When Durocher was asked what he had done as a manager to turn me from an afterthought long man to a 20-game winner, he could have hogged the credit. But he said, "I changed him from a reliever to a starter." That's all. That answer implied I had the talent and had done the work.

I felt being a bullpen man first provided a good education. I was under pressure because men were on base. Many times I couldn't afford to make a mistake, or a run would come in. There were definitely lessons about mental readiness.

Getting shut out nine times in one season is a bit much. I didn't want to make enemies out of my teammates who weren't hitting, but I was also frustrated. That season, 1968, was probably the weakest-hitting season in the history of major-league baseball, so it wasn't just the Cubs. It was an epidemic. In the American League, the Red Sox's Carl Yastrzemski hit .301, and that was good enough to win the batting title.

After I had been shut out for the fifth time, I decided to make a sacrifice to the gods, so I set our hitters' bats on fire in the outfield. I got to Wrigley Field about 8:00 AM. There was a big bat rack on a roller where guys just tossed their old, broken bats. I wasn't touching their current bats. I gathered up a bunch of these old bats and built a teepee out of them in left field on the warning track. I spread rubbing alcohol on them and tossed a match on the pile. Poof. Conflagration. The ceremonial burning of the bats.

Other players saw what I was doing, and some of them ran on the field and started yelling, "Jenks! What the hell are you doing burning up our bats?" I yelled back at them, "You guys aren't using them, so I'm burning them up!" Glenn Beckert and Don Kessinger and Billy just stood there and watched. Some of the other players were on my case, yelling, "What are you, nuts?"

I repeated, "You're not using them, so I'm using them for firewood." After a couple of minutes, I told them the truth, that the kindling was worn-out bats. "C'mon guys, I'm not really going to burn up game bats." It was a pretty good practical joke. Eventually, the fire burned out and the grounds crew shoveled dirt on it to finish it off.

It was just a prank, but someone told a *Chicago Tribune* writer, and he wrote a story that came across as serious, that I was really mad at my teammates. The headline was something like, "Jenkins Is Ticked Off, So He Burns Hitters' Bats."

Sure, I had some frustration, but that day when I was driving to the ballpark I was trying to think of something that might shake up the hitters. What gave me the idea was how Leo treated the game bats. He would walk past them in the rack, pick one up, and say, "Let's go. Let's kick up some hits from these bats."

In 1968 we really did feel as if we were going to light some fires with those bats and close in on a pennant.

10

A Harlem Globetrotter

When I was growing up in Chatham, I went from one sport to the other as the seasons changed until I became really serious about baseball. Then I just focused on baseball. I figured that it would always be that way until retired. To my great surprise, I got a fresh chance to play a sport that I always loved, but in a way I never envisioned.

I became a member of the Harlem Globetrotters.

The Globetrotters approached me to play some exhibition games for the first time in 1967. The team's general manager, George Gillette, floated the idea to a Chicago sportswriter named Wendell Smith. Smith brought the proposal to me. They wanted to use me for some of their games on their Canadian tour because I was Canadian and had a bit of a name in the athletic world. My stay with the Globetrotters was only supposed to last a week or so, but I spent parts of two off-seasons as part of the team, and I had a blast.

Everyone knew the Harlem Globetrotters—and I mean everyone in the world. The Globetrotters had been globetrotting since 1927, putting smiles on kids' and adults' faces around the United States, Canada, and dozens of other countries, for 40 years. They never lost the games they played, and they played almost every day. They had frequent-flyer miles before there were frequent-flyer miles. They also had frequent-bus miles. I was very impressed with how the Globetrotters coped with travel demands in North America, leaving after games and traveling all night for their next gig. I can't imagine how much more difficult that was when crossing international borders overseas.

The Globetrotters came to me in 1967, the year after the team founder, Abe Saperstein, died. They originally wanted me for my name, but I had enough basketball ability to impress them. They made sure of that by putting me through a tryout in a Chicago gym. I was a pretty good player in high school. When I entered high school, I was 6'1" or so, and I grew a couple of inches. We had some bigger kids than me. The highest scoring game I ever had in high school was 45 points. I was good on the fast break, and I had a good jump shot. We didn't have the three-point shot then, and I didn't take my jumpers from too far out. I dribbled inside a lot. I did well on the offensive boards, and I hit about 80 percent of my free throws.

I didn't play very much basketball after high school and before the Globetrotters. But we had a traveling team called the Cougars I played on sometimes for a couple of years when I was home in Chatham in the winter.

The funny thing is that the Cubs gave me their blessing to play basketball, but they went ballistic when I went horseback riding. They did tell me I better not get hurt. I got paid $150 a game for the Globetrotters, but that also covered my public relations work leading up to each game.

Initially, the Globetrotters used me more for publicity purposes, as part of the advance advertising team, to go ahead into larger Canadian cities to drum up support for the gate. I was originally signed to play a dozen games, but my comedy routine was popular, and they asked me to stay on for 20 games. I played throughout Canada, in Buffalo, and in Chicago. The team designed a skit just for me. I was advertised as the pitcher who gave up a home run every night. The most fun I had was playing games in Ontario, including London and Windsor. My mom and dad came to those games, and so did many other Jenkins relatives.

I sat on the bench in my Globetrotter red, white, and blue uniform, until the third quarter. My routine started without me. Mel Davis was playing the role of pitcher. Curly Neal was the catcher. Bobby Joe Mason was the umpire, and the famous showman Meadowlark Lemon was the hitter. Mel threw the ball over Meadowlark's head and then called time out. Curly shouted, "We need a real pitcher!" Meadowlark announced, "Hey, we have a famous Chicago pitcher in the crowd! Let's play a ballgame." As part of the routine, the Globetrotters coaxed me onto the court. Then I "pitched" to Meadowlark. I wound up and rolled the ball to him. One of the other players, acting as an umpire, yelled, "Strike one!" Then I threw the ball to Meadowlark. That would be strike two. On the third throw, Meadowlark swung and bashed the ball, usually into the stands for a home run. He ran around the bases, the ball was thrown home, and it got there ahead of him. Meadowlark pointed the other way as a distraction, then slid home, and was called safe. He was standing at almost halfcourt, and he finished off the routine by tossing up a long-distance hook shot. If he missed it a couple of times, I grabbed the rebound and dunked.

I stayed in the game and played real basketball the whole third quarter. Mostly I got rebounds. We traveled with the Washington Generals or the New York Americans. They were the perpetual losers to the Globetrotters, their traveling opponents. Red Klotz was there, and he organized the other team for years and years. A lot of the guys on those teams asked for autographs because I was a baseball player, but they knew I wasn't a star on the Globetrotters. Meadowlark was the star.

The Globetrotters had their staple of comedy routines that people all over the world came to recognize. They also had some temporary skits, like mine. But they were all very good basketball players.

Over the years, the Globetrotters have featured a large number of guest players, some of whom played entire seasons. Wilt Chamberlain played for the Globetrotters instead of playing his final season at Kansas. Lynette Woodard was the first woman to play for the Globetrotters. Bob Gibson, my old pitching rival, played for the Globetrotters. The great Connie Hawkins, who ended up in the Hall of Fame, played for the Globetrotters, too, early in his career. When we played in Detroit, Willie Horton of the Tigers sat on the bench.

In between the routines, the Globetrotters played some good basketball. They had to play well enough to win almost all of their games. In one game in Montreal, I scored 10 points. That opened their eyes a little bit to the fact that I had the ability to play some serious ball. I think that game led to my return engagement going way beyond Canada. The second off-season I played with the Globetrotters, I played in 85 games.

I had a lot of fun with the Globetrotters. I got to play basketball in Madison Square Garden. We played the Cow Palace in San Francisco, at UCLA, and some other big college venues. I probably played basketball in all of the Big Ten college gyms and out West in major hockey arenas. We did the magic circle, moving the ball around as they played "Sweet Georgia Brown," and that was a thrill.

We played one game in Saskatchewan, and we never dribbled the ball one time in the game. The floor was wet. Using portable floors could be tough. It was a low scoring game, maybe 48-35, but the Globetrotters did all of their "reams" and nobody fell. It was something. In one place, the arena was unheated, and it was 17 degrees inside the building. We wore sweatpants.

Playing with the Globetrotters was like being the Pied Piper. From the moment the bus pulled into town with "The World Famous Harlem Globetrotters" written on the side, kids would follow us. People banged on the door. Darn right they were world famous.

I played with a good group of guys. Meadowlark Lemon was the headliner. He was the chief clown, and he was the leader in the skits. But away from the court he kept to himself. He didn't clown around. Later he became a minister. He has his own church in the Phoenix area. He's got his own boys club. He has a circuit where he preaches. I still see him. He comes to my golf outings for charity in Arizona. We talk from time to time. He's very down-to-earth.

The first tour was a short one and mostly in Canada. When the Globetrotters came back to me for 1968, it was a much bigger tour. We did all of the same Canadian venues and more, including Hawaii. We played a game on an aircraft carrier. Howard Cosell was there, and he interviewed us for a segment on *Wide World of Sports*. They filmed most of the game. Most of what they showed was Curly Neal, who was a marvel dribbling the ball. They showed his great skill in dodging defenders and dribbling circles around them. It really was amazing to watch. A year after that a cartoon was made about the Globetrotters, aimed at kids. They used five characters, Meadowlark, Curly, Showboat Hall, Mel Davis, and Jackie Jackson.

Meadowlark was the glitzy showman. He was the point man on the reams. There was one routine where he went into the stands to bring out a girl who was very fair skinned and had red hair. He hugged her, and then all of a sudden he pulled a bra out of his shirt or shorts, and this female blushed redder than her hair. One of the other players would yell as loud as he could, "Is that her bra?" You know, to make sure she was even more embarrassed.

The Globetrotters kept a lot of the same routines going for years. People saw them, knew they were coming, and they still laughed. There was always the famous water-bucket ream. At one point during the game, a player ran around chasing Meadowlark with a bucket of "water." Meadowlark ran this way and that way and always led the player near the fans in the front of the stands. The player gave the contents of the water bucket the heave-ho, Meadowlark ducked, and the stuff spilled out on a fan. But it was just confetti. The crowd thought the fan would get soaked. Then, late in the game, the Trotters reenacted the same scenario. The bucket, the chase, Meadowlark ducking, all the same. Only this time there really was water in the bucket, and it splashed all over a referee. Essentially, they got the audience twice with the same trick in the same game.

Curly was completely bald, like Michael Jordan, and he had a ream where he kicked the ball through the hoop from halfcourt. It would go through the hoop so fast, just dropping from the sky. People went crazy when they saw things like that. A lot of what was behind the success of the Globetrotter routines was that people saw them and thought, *Oh, man, that can't be happening.*

Jackie Jackson was an incredible leaper. "Jumping Jackie," he was called. We played in gymnasiums where we put a quarter on top of the backboard, 12 feet off the floor, and he would jump up and grab it. He'd have his chin above the rim and take it off the backboard with his hand. He had huge hands. Jackie was the first guy I ever saw who dunked two basketballs at the same time. He did it in Buffalo at Niagara University, where Calvin Murphy played. Calvin averaged more than 30 points a game during his college career before he starred in the NBA, but not everybody remembers that of all things he was a champion baton twirler. When the Globetrotters played there in the 1960s, Calvin came out and spun his baton. He did an act.

The Globetrotters had been around for four decades when I joined them. They had visited more countries than any diplomat. They were known everywhere, even where English wasn't spoken. What they did crossed barriers. The Globetrotters were the greatest ambassadors for the United States. And they always wore red, white, and blue, so you knew where they came from. They were ambassadors for basketball, for entertainment, and for the U.S.

Playing with the Globetrotters wasn't that taxing. It was mostly fun, and with the Globetrotters I never lost. That was a nice incentive as an athlete. I saved the yearbooks from the two years I played with the Globetrotters. I kept my jersey, too. I would have loved to have that silk jacket they wore. I don't know why I didn't ask for it. One thing that the Globetrotters have that I have saved and really appreciate is an alumni badge and an alumni card that read "Harlem Globetrotters."

I remember all of the Globetrotters fondly, including Meadowlark, Curly, Mel, Jackie, and Bobby Joe Mason. Bobby Joe passed away a couple of years ago from a heart attack. Some of the older players aren't doing so well. I have a bunch of pictures of all the guys. It was a special time for me. The Globetrotters made it possible for me to play basketball on a much bigger stage than I ever did in Chatham. It was a privilege, and I was lucky to be invited into their world for a short period of time.

I admit that any time I hear the song "Sweet Georgia Brown" I think of the Harlem Globetrotters. I bet that a lot of people do because it's their signature music, but I can think back and remember that I was part of it. I was a member of the Harlem Globetrotters and not only listened to the song in full uniform, but participated in the magic circle.

11

1969

Even before the 1969 season began, we expected it to be a big year for the Cubs. Leo Durocher's plan was in place. His winning attitude had taken root in the organization. We knew we had the talent to contend for the National League pennant. And his eminence, Mr. Cub, Ernie Banks, announced, "The Cubs will shine in '69."

He was right.

That was a Cubs team that is still special to fans. We had a lot of great ballplayers on the team, and we had a good run. For most of the season, it looked as if we were going to be the first Cubs team since 1945 to win the pennant. I had 42 starts that year and finished 21-15. It was the third straight season that I won 20 games. I really did have something going. The Cubs had something going, too. What a solid team we had. Ernie Banks at first, Glenn Beckert at second, Don Kessinger at short, Ron Santo at third, and Randy Hundley catching. They were all All-Stars. That was terrific.

Almost right from the first game of the season, things felt different. I was the Opening Day pitcher against the Phillies. There were 40,796 fans at Wrigley Field. It was not my best outing. We built a 5-1 lead, but Don Money ate me up that day. He knocked in five runs. But in the bottom of the eleventh inning, Willie Smith hit a pinch-hit, two-run, walk-off homer to give us a 7-6 victory, and the crowd went crazy. We moved into first place by April 15, and we stayed there for five months. People were actually making records singing about the Cubs. It was wild. There were posters being made.

We came into the 1969 season with absolute faith in Leo Durocher. The Cubs had been regulars in the cellar until he came along, and we believed that he and we were on the right path. We felt Leo was a big part of the Cubs' revival. There was even a preseason sportswriters poll that picked the Cubs to win the division. I don't know how long it had been since the Cubs had been picked to win anything.

There was a special occasion on June 29 when the Cubs declared it Billy Williams Day. It was actually a doubleheader, and Billy really tore it up that day. He also broke the National League record by playing in his 895th and 896th games in a row. Williams was called "Sweet Swinging Billy Williams," but he actually could have been called "Old Reliable" Billy Williams because he was there to play every day. Billy's record eventually extended to playing 1,117 straight games before he took a day off. Billy was presented with an automobile and a boat, among other gifts, and he showed why he was so popular by slamming two triples, two doubles, and a single that day.

On August 19, Kenny Holtzman pitched a no-hitter to beat the Braves, and he did it without striking out a single batter. Everything was going our way. Before the end of the month, the team got the word that it was okay to print playoff tickets. But the Mets got hotter and hotter. By early September, New York was within five games.

It was great coming to the ballpark all summer. We were winning, and winning handily. And other times, we might be trailing in the seventh inning or so and make a comeback. Billy Williams or Jim Hickman would hit a home run. Al Spangler got a lot of pinch-hits for us. We were a team to be reckoned with, and we had a nine–game lead. All of a sudden, the defense, the offense, and the pitching waned. It was a combination of all three. And the Mets got hot. They were phenomenal. They couldn't lose, and we went into a slump. We just couldn't compete. We'd go into St. Louis, and they would jump on us. Cincinnati jumped on us. The Phillies, too.

The big series that haunted us began on September 8. We went into Shea Stadium to play two games against the Mets. Bill Hands's first pitch to Tommie Agee was high and inside to send a message, and he knocked him down. But Agee came back and hit a home run two innings later. There was a tight play at the plate in the sixth inning when it was 2–2. Agee was involved in that, too. He slid in, and Hundley tagged him. We were sure he was out, but the umpire called Agee safe. We felt that the three blind mice could have called Agee out, but we were playing in Shea Stadium, so he was safe. We lost that game 3–2, and that cut our lead to 1½ games.

The Mets cut another game off the lead the next day. I got beat by Tom Seaver easily, 7–1.

That was a bittersweet year. It did feel like one that got away. It could have been us in the Series instead of the Mets. We just didn't get it done at the end of the season. There was a lot of feeling that if we had won it in 1969, we would have kept on winning and probably won in 1970, too. I thought we had an even better team in 1970.

There was an awful lot of criticism later that Durocher should have used his bench more later in the season. We played all day games, and there was a feeling that the Cubs were more sapped of energy than other teams because of it. But that was not Leo's way. He picked his guys and went with them. He played the best guys every day. If you were tired, you were expected to go to him and tell him, but what regular was going to do that? We had a good bench, but Leo didn't use it very much. From about the middle of August on, I sensed that Leo wanted the regulars to play every inning of every game. He could taste the pennant and was hungry to win another one after all of his success in Brooklyn and New York. It would be the capstone of his career if he could raise the lowly Cubs from the basement to the National League pennant. Durocher picked up the pressure on the regulars, but he didn't give them any relief. Durocher told players to come to him if they felt they needed a break, but he really didn't want to hear that. He wanted everyone to suck it up.

Leo got more and more superstitious, too. If we won the day before, he wanted the bat rack positioned the same way. He wanted the same player sitting next to him in the dugout who had been sitting next to him for the last win.

After a win when Ron Santo spontaneously jumped up along the third-base line and clicked his heels together and the fans went nuts over it, Durocher asked Santo if he could do it every game. Durocher wanted him to reprise the act every game after that. The Cubs fans loved it, but opposing players thought Ronnie was trying to show them up. The fact was that such enthusiasm came naturally to Ronnie all of the time, and it was just the expression of his happiness when he did it the first time. Then there was the black cat incident. Ronnie was on deck when a black cat ran out from the stands at Shea Stadium during that September series, circled him as he warmed up swinging his bats, and then disappeared. For the doom and gloom club, the black cat was just another sign that our luck was turning sour.

The 1969 season, because it was our best, was the focal point of that group of guys. That was an incredibly closely knit team, and 40 years later a lot of us are still friends. The nucleus of the team stayed together under Leo, and it should have because there were a lot of very good players. We had grown up together as young players. One of the guys added to the mix who was a big help was Gene Oliver as a backup catcher and pinch-hitter. Oliver was nearing the end of his career—that was his last season—and was there to provide a breather. Gene, who was a great guy, was so happy to come over to the Cubs because he thought we were going to be champs. After we had been in first place for months and started to lose, he said if we didn't win the pennant he would jump off the 100-story Hancock Building that opened that year. We didn't win, and Gene didn't jump. Not even with a parachute. That was one bet he didn't pay off.

That year, Leo, who previously had been married to actress Laraine Day and always ran with a Hollywood crowd, married Lynne Walker Goldblatt, a department store heiress in Chicago. His new stepson was going to a boys' camp over the summer, and Leo took a few days off from managing. He turned the team over to coach Pete Reiser. It was kind of unbelievable that he had to drive this eight- or nine-year-old to camp and couldn't manage the Cubs. There was a big article in the papers about Leo's being absent.

After the disaster against the Mets, we moved on to Philadelphia and lost 6–2. The Mets won a doubleheader from the Expos. That put New York into first place. We had held first for 155 days, but when we lost it, we never got it back. The Mets just pulled away. We finished 92-70, and the Mets won the National League East Division by eight games. The Mets finished so strongly they won 100 games. The Mets steamrolled through the rest of the regular season schedule and then upset the Baltimore Orioles in the World Series. The Mets just played better. You've got to give them that, their due. They just beat us.

Durocher got a lot of criticism when the season was over. There were suggestions that he was losing it. We were on the verge of winning, but it just didn't happen. Leo was getting older, but I don't think he was losing it. He was still sharp. He was making the right moves. We had some problems with the bullpen, and some of the guys might have been a little bit tired, but it wasn't as if he was throwing untested rookies out there from the bullpen in the pressure of the pennant race and saying, "Hey, do it." Leo wasn't that type of manager. Leo Durocher was good for the Cubs. In a few years we had improved from 59 wins to 92 wins. Attendance in 1969 was 1,674,993. That's insignificant compared to what the Cubs draw at Wrigley Field now, but at the time it was a team attendance record.

Durocher was good for me, too. He recognized the potential in me to be a starting pitcher. I went from an unproven rookie to a veteran who, by the end of the 1969 season, had won 20 or more games three straight years. I got a lot of wins, and I had the confidence of the organization.

My life changed away from the ballpark, too. When my wife Kathy and I first went to Chicago, we had just gotten married, but we didn't have a family. Pretty soon we had three little girls. Winning 20 games each season made me a popular athlete in town, too. I was recognized all over. In restaurants, going out for a walk, playing golf, everywhere, people knew me. It was always, "Hey, Fergie," like one of the guys. I'm a people person, and I loved talking to the fans. I went from being part of a couple to having a family at home, and from a player in an organization where he grew up going to another where it became family. The Cubs organization was great at the time and was like a family.

It really is amazing that a lot of us from that team stay in touch. A big part of that was Randy Hundley creating his Cubs fantasy camp in the early 1980s. Randy was correct in reading the sports market and realizing that older Cub fans would love to have a chance to meet the old players and spend time getting instruction from them on the field. What neither Randy nor any of us realized at first was that it would be just as much fun for us to get back together as it was for the fans who met us.

Over the years I have attended the camps with Billy Williams and Ernie Banks, Glenn Beckert and Don Kessinger, and, of course, Randy. We spend a lot of time enjoying each other's company, and when we put the uniform on, it reminds us of how proud we were to be members of the Cubs together in the 1960s.

12

Inside Pitching

The Cubs were winning. I was in the majors. I was winning. Things were going great in Chicago. We felt for sure we were on the cusp of capturing a pennant. I was popular in the community. I related to the fans. It was a fun time all around.

I know some players like to keep a higher degree of privacy, but I enjoyed mingling with the fans.

After I noticed that Ernie Banks had done it, I got a vanity license plate that read "FJ31" for "Fergie Jenkins" and my uniform number. In so many ways, I felt I was at the top of my game. I was a three-time, 20-game winner, and I believed I had turned the corner from thrower to pitcher. That is a big step for any pitcher, especially young pitchers who don't even know the difference. You start as a thrower and evolve into a pitcher.

By 1972 I even coauthored a little book with a writer named Dave Fisher called *Inside Pitching*. The book was aimed at young pitchers and focused on pitching techniques and my advice for how to succeed on the mound. In the preface I said, "The pitcher is the most important player on the field. The first time I stepped onto the pitcher's mound, I felt awkward and out of place. I knew what I wanted to do, but my body wouldn't cooperate. So I worked at it, and pitching eventually became a natural movement for my body. I could throw hard, and I had control, but I didn't really begin to learn what pitching was all about until I entered professional baseball."

To make this instructional book relevant for even the youngest beginners, I talked about basic fundamentals, introducing kids to the ball, the glove, the pitching rubber, and the mound itself. If you are a parent or a coach who is dealing with a youngster, you can't assume that the youngster you are dealing with knows anything about anything. He may have formed some vague ideas from watching television, but he may not know the proper techniques.

Most kids are simply going to run out to the pitching mound, turn around, and start throwing. A pitcher examines the mound itself. It is his office. I believe in making a careful inspection tour of the mound. I walk around it several times. I look at the ground. I want to see if there are rocks anywhere, if there are bumps or uneven spots I wouldn't expect to see, and if there are any hazards that might cause me to trip or slip when I complete my pitching motion. If it has been rainy and there is a muddy spot, I try to build a dry spot where I can land so I won't slip when I release the ball.

The pitching rubber on the mound at Wrigley Field measures 24 inches long by six inches wide. If you are in a rudimentary playground, they might not have a rubber. If you are pitching in the backyard, you might want to make your own pitching rubber. When I was growing up in Canada, kids built their own. We would nail a piece of an old tire into the ground and use that.

If you are a serious baseball player, careful thought should be given to selecting a glove. A good glove can cost $100, so it is an important investment. My first glove was a hunk of leather that my dad had used. He cut the center out of the pocket because he said it gave him better control fielding balls. But every time I caught a ball in that glove, it hurt my hand. Glove manufacturing companies sign up major-league ballplayers for endorsement deals and sell replica gloves with the players' facsimile signatures on them. In the early 1970s there was a Ferguson Jenkins model glove. But every player is different. It is nice if you want to buy a glove because you are a fan of a particular player, but it is not always practical.

Fit is the most important thing. Young people should have a glove that allows enough room for finger movement but is not so big it will fall off or prevent them from having glove control with one hand. No glove should be so small it cramps fingers. And no glove should be so large that the player has to grow into as he ages. Over the years, fancier, more colorful models have been introduced. That's just for fun. I had a blue glove at one point. The color, however, is the least important thing about a glove.

It is important to be able to field your position well. A pitcher can help himself if he is quick to react to line drives or ground balls and can field bunts. We did a lot of pitching drills, playing pepper, to help hand-eye coordination and produce fast reactions. I led the league in fielding a couple of times at my position. It's not so easy to do because, after you release the ball, your body is falling out of control. When you fall off the pitching rubber as a right-hander to the first-base side all of the time, you're not going to field balls up the middle.

Jim Bunning and Bob Gibson came off the rubber hard, but they had good recovery time. I've seen the Kerry Wood fall off the mound, put his glove behind his back, and field the ball. I thought, *Damn, how lucky is that?* That glove is there for a reason, and sometimes it's like a magnet. The ball goes right into your glove. The flip side of those occasions is that the ball sometimes gets hit right back at you. I was lucky. In 22 years of pitching, I only got hit a couple of times. Leron Lee, the father of Derrek Lee with the Cubs, hit a line drive off my thigh and knocked me off the hill. Boom, boom. I got a standing ovation because I got up. Those plays are always scary. It happened in a split second. The ball was on me. I had time to think, *Oh, my God.* I had a couple of balls hit on my leg and my feet, but I was fortunate not to be hit around the head.

One time Willie Stargell of the Pirates hit a line drive so hard up the middle that I heard it go by. If you are throwing the ball in the high 80s or low 90s, the reaction time is a split second. Sometimes it comes back harder.

Something I learned is that the pitcher is really the guy in charge of the game. Nothing can happen until he decides he is ready. Fans might be shouting to hurry up and throw the ball already, but that's just background noise. The pitcher can't be pressured by that. Believe it or not, you are even more important than a television commercial. The TV executives can stop the game, but only the pitcher can start it again.

Getting ready to throw is a mental and physical process. It makes no sense to throw the pitch if you think the batter is going to hit it. Readiness is critical. Before you swing your hands back into your windup, you should be totally confident that you know which pitch you are going to throw. You should know what the strategic situation is, where your fielders are positioned, and what the batter is expecting.

It is important for the pitcher to think ahead. He should be thinking what he will do if the batter hits a grounder to short. He should be thinking what he will throw next if the batter swings and misses. He should be thinking what his next pitch will be if he misses for ball one. It is also useful to hide the ball from the prying eyes of hitters, to protect from view how you are placing your fingers on the ball. Next to pitchers, hitters are the smartest baseball players on a team. Don't help them! You're not a charitable organization, and you don't have to give away any information to the hitter. When you're on the mound, the ball should be held in your glove in precisely the same way every time.

When I went into my windup, I put my hands together and raised my arms directly over my head. I raised my left leg and jackknifed it at the knee. Then I took the ball from the glove and brought my right arm around behind my torso. As I did that, I kicked my left leg out straight. Dropping the ball behind my body, I planted the left foot, then I reared back, right arm slightly below my shoulders, and brought my hand back, bent the wrist, and whipped my arm forward to release the pitch. There are basically three angles of delivery: full overhand, three-quarters overhand, and sidearm. Very few pitchers use a fourth, the submarine style that is almost underhanded. My delivery position of choice was three-quarters. That felt the most natural. Pitchers have to experiment, to try all options, to determine what is best for them. Your arm, as well as results, will tell you what's right. If your arm doesn't like the way you are throwing, it will be strained and cause you some pain.

It is nice to believe that if you can throw 100 miles per hour no batter will ever touch your fastball. Certainly anyone who is blessed with such a raw gift of power is fortunate. But the most important part of successful pitching is varying speed and location. It's great to throw the ball in a blur, but you can be more effective by mixing in changeups. Location, putting the ball where you want it to go, and movement, making the ball dance to your tune, is what helps young pitchers turn into old pitchers.

Before I threw a pitch, I developed a long checklist of do's and don'ts, and one of the key things I focused on was self-belief. I didn't want to go to the mound without thinking I could get every hitter out. I would talk to myself and say, "Fergie, this team simply cannot beat you." Confidence is tremendously important. If you don't have it, you'll be afraid to challenge hitters, and you'll end up in the showers.

Once I had myself psyched up, I wanted to see if I could somehow psych out the batter. These are major-league hitters, the best in the world, and they wouldn't have reached the top of the game if they didn't have skills, too. They come to the plate with their own goals and game plan. They are out there to beat you. Chances are, especially if you have been around for a little while, the hitters know what you throw and what tendencies you have. They are trying to out-think you. So it becomes a game of counter-intelligence, sort of like spy versus spy.

Over the years, some pitchers took their acts beyond the field. They developed a persona that would make batters think they were crazy. Bill Faul, who was with the Cubs in 1965 and 1966, definitely took this path. He introduced hypnosis to the clubhouse and told people when he put himself under he was a better pitcher. He also wore No. 13, defying superstition. Ryne Duren, a relief pitcher of the 1960s for the New York Yankees, wore very thick glasses. Everyone said they were as dense as the bottom of Coca-Cola bottles. Duren had a terrific fastball, and often when he came into a game he threw his first pitch completely wild. The ball would sail over the head of a batter at high velocity. Then to add to the image of a pitcher out of control, the Yankee catcher, Elston Howard, or Yogi Berra, would shrug and say they didn't know where the next pitch was going. Duren played with the batters' minds. After that little trick, all they wanted to do was get back to the bench alive.

One simple tool a pitcher can use to keep a hitter off-balance is to shake off the sign from his catcher. The pitcher and catcher may be on the same wavelength, but if they switch from sign to sign it may get the batter wondering what's going on.

A variation of the Ryne Duren approach was being more direct with a brushback pitch, or a purpose pitch. If the batter is crowding the plate, he is daring you to throw inside. He wants to force you into throwing to the outside corner and he'll be waiting to powder the ball. You can't have that. You can't surrender any of the plate. You have to take him up on the dare and move him off the plate by throwing 90 miles an hour in tight. If he doesn't hit the dirt and drop his bat, you haven't gotten the message across. In the 1960s, with fearless, confident, fastball hurlers like Bob Gibson and Don Drysdale around, a hitter couldn't dig in. The hitter knew those guys had no remorse about hitting them. That was all part of the game. Batters did not get the protection from umpires that they do now. Baseball has evolved so that it is a crime to even look at a batter with a squint or a snarl, never mind actually hit him with a pitch. This makes life so much easier for the batter. A brushback pitch let the batter know you meant business and that he was not going to get anything for free off of you. Brushing a hitter back is different from throwing a beanball. A beanball is illegal to throw, and it is thrown with the intent to hurt a batter. That should not be part of the pitcher's arsenal.

Every once in a while you'll see a pitcher who has a good-sized belly in the majors. That used to happen more often. I like to think I was one of the best-conditioned pitchers out there when I played due to the years of off-season work I did with Gene Dziadura. But pitchers then generally did not spend much time working out away from the ballpark. Now it seems that's all they do year-round, whether it's running, lifting weights, or doing exercises. I thought it was an advantage being in shape. David Wells, who was a hefty guy, pitched a perfect game with a pretty good-sized belly, though, so maybe there is no hard-and-fast rule.

Because my father was a chef, I learned how to cook, and I learned a little bit about nutrition. He taught me to prepare food. I was in the kitchen a lot with my dad when he prepared food. He made everything. I ate a lot of steak, a lot of chicken. I had liver and onions. My dad prepared certain types of vegetables. There were a lot of fish dishes and pasta, like spaghetti and lasagna. I'm a decent cook. I never worried about getting fat because I have a good metabolism.

I might have trained harder than anyone else when I was playing because of the early influence and assistance from Gene. I also was in a different environment. Being in Canada I didn't know what other young athletes were doing to get ready for the baseball season because our season was so short and I was not exposed to a lot of others outside the immediate area.

Pitching hard and pitching inside were things I learned in the minor leagues. No hitter wants to get embarrassed by the fact that you are using that tool to push him off the plate, but even if it meant changing their footwork or the angle of their eyes when you threw, those little things mattered.

There were some hitters in my era that weren't going to give an inch. Frank Robinson, the Hall of Famer, was one, and sometimes he got hit by a pitch. When we hit someone, they just ran down to first. Now if you hit somebody, they all want to fight. They want to start a riot. It's just because they are usually so protected by the umpire. I never hit a guy in the head. I hit guys in the shoulder blade, the butt, or the legs. I never hit them in the head or the neck. That was out. I hit guys in the ribs. It takes their breath away. It even makes it tough to run down to first. There is a huge difference between a brushback pitch and a beanball.

A beaning is malicious. You're trying to take somebody's career away by beaning them, and that's not what the game's all about. Pushing the guy off the plate is strategy, making him feel uncomfortable. Batters wear shin guards and elbow pads and things like that now, so much that it's like armor. These guys dress like goalies in hockey now. Barry Bonds was extreme. David Ortiz. Some guys who have never been thrown at in the course of their careers throw their hands up, and there are a lot of really small bones in the hand, so they get their hand busted. Then they're out for six weeks.

Major-league baseball players are probably better conditioned now than they have been in the history of the sport, and the hitters probably get more protection from the way the rules are enforced than any other time, too.

13

After the '69 Collapse

After the 1969 run at the pennant, the Cubs had confidence. We thought we would bounce back and take the pennant in 1970. We still thought we had the players and the lineup to do it.

Maybe it was the way we lost, but we never regained the spark from 1969. The Cubs of 1970 were pretty good, but our record of 84-78 was no better than it had been when we were starting to build the club in 1968. We finished second by five games, but it wasn't like 1969. For the fourth year in a row, I won 20 games, finishing 22-16.

At that point I was probably at the top of my game. I was intimidating hitters, especially right-handers. I got right-handers out all of the time. I got ahead of the hitters, and if a batter let me get ahead, I got ahead quick and got control of the at-bat. I turned a lot of clubs into first-ball hitters. I tried to present an image of a big guy on the mound who was there to get you out. I'd knock people off the plate.

Bringing that attitude, that mood, I think, helped the attitude of the team. The guys knew I was going to give them a good opportunity to win. Guys played hard for me. I tried to look as confident as possible on the mound. I didn't want to be too brash. I didn't really believe in tooting my own horn, but I wanted everyone to know that I felt I was capable of winning.

Once you start winning and you win on a consistent basis, the challenge is to keep it going. I knew I could win. I wanted to keep on winning. I didn't want to lose that intensity. I tried to stay as intense as possible. So each season I came in with the focus that I wanted to win 20 or more games. I used to look at the schedule and check off every fourth day for my starts. I'd get six starts this month and maybe get seven starts the next month. I knew I was going to get 35-plus starts. I told myself the number-one factor was not to get hurt. I might get hit with a ball, but I never had a sore arm. If my arm was tight, I used to take Tylenol. That was my remedy.

I just kept winning my 20 games, every year, for six seasons in a row. Now that some time has passed and the sport has changed with pitchers getting fewer starts, I don't think anybody is going to do that again. You've got to let these young men pitch longer in games. If they only get 28 or 33 starts, the odds are against them winning 20 games. There are going to be too many no-decisions. There will be some games they get taken out too early. There will be some games when the pitch count gets up there and the manager removes them. I don't really know what the most number of pitches I ever threw in a game was, but it was probably 140 or 150. My arm is still attached.

We never did win a pennant when I was with the Cubs, but we had a lot of great guys and great players. It was a privilege to play with Ernie Banks. The man played his entire career with the Cubs and hit 512 home runs. I roomed with Ernie on the road for two and a half years. He was a joyful individual. Ernie always had the reputation of being an energetic individual. He is Mr. Cub. He's like the Cubs' ambassador.

Ernie and I got along great as roommates. We didn't fight over TV channels or anything like that. We went to dinner. His family knew my family. I knew his. I thought what he brought to the game was a recognizable individual who was all class. Ernie was always in a good mood. He never got mad at anybody, except sometimes himself when he wasn't happy about what he did in a game. If you're a ballplayer and you go 0-for-4, sure you get mad at yourself for not performing better. But Ernie was on a pretty even keel most of the time.

Ernie made up those rhymes about how it was going to be a Cubs pennant year. He did it every year. He would still like to come back to the team and be president of the Cubs before he retires altogether. It could happen.

Billy Williams was my best friend on the Cubs. Billy and I were fishing and hunting buddies. I admired Billy for his capabilities. He was such a good hitter, but he was kind of in the shadow of Ernie. He handled it well. Billy had the best swing of anybody I ever saw. He knew his role. He played hard. He threw well enough to lead the league in assists. Ernie was Mr. Cub, but if Ernie was not there, then maybe Billy Williams would have been Mr. Cub. Billy was an iron-clad individual. He played every day, even when he was hurt. He's another individual who is a class act.

Ron Santo was a hard-nosed player. He was meant to play. He sweated and played down and dirty at third base, giving it all, day in and day out. He also played when he was hurt. One game he got hit in the face with the ball, but he played two days later with his eye still bruised. Ron just went out there and wanted to win more than anybody else. He was a die-hard. Ron wore his emotions on his sleeve as a player and still does as a broadcaster. He broadcasts the same way he played. People portray Ron Santo as a Cub to the core. You can hear it in his voice when he's broadcasting with Pat Hughes. He's joyful when the Cubs come up with base hits and they win. He's what they call a "homer," but he loves the Cubs.

Ron has battled diabetes and has lost both his legs, but he has a heart bigger than Wrigley Field. It takes a lot to battle back from that, but he's proven he's capable of doing it. It took a while for us to know that Ron was a diabetic and that he was taking insulin shots. I think it takes a special individual who has been battling that type of illness and playing at the level he played at all that time. It takes a lot of intestinal fortitude.

Kenny Holtzman had a great arm, and he was a great teammate. He had a good career. He got matched up against Sandy Koufax, it seemed, all of the time, and I don't know how many of those games any pitcher was going to win. He had a good streak of winning a lot of games in Chicago and pitched two no-hitters for the Cubs. Then, when he went to Oakland, he got to pitch in several World Series. In 1968 Kenny had the strangest season because he was in the reserves. He got called up, and he'd miss three weeks, then come back and win a game. He'd miss two or three weeks and come back and win again. Kenny enjoyed himself as a Cub. We'd go to dinner, sit around and play cards, get together if we wanted to talk baseball. We played poker or hearts.

Don Kessinger made himself into a good ballplayer. He taught himself to switch-hit while in the big leagues, which is kind of unheard of nowadays. He had a great arm and was an All-Star shortstop. He was a great lead-off hitter who could steal bases. He was a star college basketball player. We used to sit around in the locker room and talk about fielding position when facing certain hitters. He knew how I liked to pitch, and he picked my brains about playing hitters a certain way.

Glenn Beckert was another hard-nosed player, but he was a funny guy. Leo Durocher nicknamed him "Bruno." Glenn would play jokes. He stepped on people's feet all of the time in the dugout or the locker room. He bummed cigarettes. He'd bump into you and go, "Hi, Jimmy," even when he knew you weren't named Jimmy. He phones me all of the time on my birthday, and he was the best man at my third wedding in Oklahoma.

Randy Hundley was our catcher, and he caught all of the time. He set records for catching the most number of games in a season. Randy didn't want to rest. He is a very loyal guy. He was very down-to-earth and a very good friend. We called Randy "Shucks" because he never used profanity. He never swore. He'd say "shucks" or "darn it" or "dang blame it." He said things that made you chuckle. Randy was always ready to play. He called a good game, and he was always back there behind the dish. One year he caught 160 games. Now catchers go for 10 games in a row and they need five days off.

Bill Hands was a great pitcher with the Cubs when I was there. He won 20 games in 1969 and won 18 the next year. He had a great slider. Bill went toe to toe with a lot of other good pitchers. He didn't get the notoriety because he was behind me and Kenny, but Bill could flat-out pitch.

Jim Hickman was a great teammate. He was a clutch hitter and just loved to play in big games. He played several positions, but whenever he was called on, he went out and was always capable of doing it.

Ted "Fritz" Savage once sat down in the dugout where Durocher liked to sit. Durocher came up to him and said, "What are you doing here? Go down to the bullpen." Savage ran out of there and said, "He scares the snot out of me."

Another time, Lee Thomas, who was our number-one left-handed pinch-hitter, was sent to the on-deck circle by Durocher. But all of the time he was swinging the bat and warming up, Durocher was having a conversation with himself like he was talking to an audience. He said, "I'm sending him [Thomas] up there. I know he's gonna pop up. I don't why I sent him in. He's gonna pop up. Oh, don't pop up." And on the first pitch Thomas hit a pop-up. Durocher yelled, "I knew he was gonna do that!" Guys on the bench were all laughing, and when Thomas came back, he broke the bat and wondered why the heck everyone was laughing. Someone told him what Leo had been saying, and Thomas looked at Leo and said, "Why the hell did you send me up there if you knew I was gonna pop up?"

We were in Montreal once to play the Expos. We had just been swept three straight by Atlanta, and Leo said we all had to be in our rooms in Montreal by 1:00 AM. He sent the coaches, Pete Reiser and Joe Becker, around to knock on doors and do bed checks. Well, they did the tour, and 19 out of 25 guys were not in their rooms. The next day, Leo had a team meeting and went ballistic. He said he was fining everyone and expected to have checks on his desk in his office after the game. I can't remember if I was one of them or not, but I probably was. Montreal was a good town for me. I'm Canadian. Nineteen guys missed curfew.

Leo was the type of guy who, if he caught you drinking in the hotel bar, he didn't want you to try to sneak out. He said, "If I walk into the bar, buy me a round. Don't be walking out without buying me a round." Really, Leo had very few rules. His pet peeve was that he didn't want people smoking, above all, during a team meeting.

A funny thing happened when Johnny Callison came over to the Cubs in 1970. Callison was an excellent outfielder, but Durocher liked to position his guys. He usually waved to them and sometimes he waved a towel to show them whether to move left or right. Well, it happened to be a rainy day, and the roof of the dugout at Wrigley Field was leaking after a rain delay. Leo always stood in front of the bat rack with the wall right behind him where there was a leak. So Leo was standing there knocking water off here and there with the towel, and Johnny Callison was running back and forth in the outfield. When Callison came back to the dugout, he stormed up to Leo and said, "God damn it, Skip, where the hell do you want me to play? You're running me all over the damn place."

The dugout in the Astrodome had about eight phones. Not only did it have a direct line to the bullpen, but the press box and wherever else. There was probably a hot line to a pizza shop. Leo hated all of that. We were in the middle of a tense series with the Astros when suddenly a phone started ringing. Leo picked up a phone and nobody was there. A phone rang again and nobody was there. Leo took a fungo bat and knocked all of those phones off the wall.

In 1969 Willie McCovey of the Giants was the Most Valuable Player in the National League. He was terrific. He couldn't do anything wrong, and that included hitting me. It started in spring training in Arizona. He was killing right-handed pitchers. I opened up against San Francisco, and I gave up a two-run homer to Willie. He got a couple of hits, and they won the game.

A month later, we were playing the Giants at Wrigley, and we had the same result. He got a couple of hits, and I lost the game. We had to go back out to San Francisco to play another series, and I was rooming with Ernie. In the afternoon, as we were getting ready to go to Candlestick Park, the phone rang. Ernie answered it and said it was for me. It was the concierge from downstairs and he said, "Your car is here." I turned to Ernie and said, "Ernie, did you order a car?" He said, "No, no, no, find out what it's all about." So I told the concierge we didn't order a car and he said, "Oh, the car's for Mr. Jenkins from Mr. McCovey. He said he wants to make sure that you get to the ballpark on time." Pretty funny. So I took the ride. I laughed, but I was a little bit put out.

Ernie and I took the car to the park, and when we got there, the Giants pitcher was sitting outside. I walked over and told him, "Tell Stretch that he's going 0-for-3 tonight." I told Randy Hundley that when he called the pitches to even let Willie know what was coming. Willie went 0-for-3 that night.

If you think I was frustrated by Willie McCovey's tear against me that year, at least I was giving up all those hard hits to a Hall of Famer. Nobody gloats about getting big hits more than a pitcher does, though, because it's unexpected. I was always a good hitting pitcher, but it was not my main job. That was gravy. In 1971 I hit six home runs, two in one game against Montreal. Bill Stoneman, who had been a Cub a couple of years prior, started, and I drove in three or four runs off him. The position players always tease you, saying stuff like, "Fergie, taking extra batting practice tomorrow?" But I had the answer for them. I said, "Oh, I don't need to. I'm a pretty good hitter."

Leo Durocher would speak his mind on the bench, on the plane, and in the clubhouse. He was the leader of the club and he let you know it. There wasn't any getting around it. It was his team, and he ruled it with an iron hand. He wanted to win. He wanted the team to win, and unfortunately we came close, but we didn't get there. He would voice his opinion about how we were playing all of the time. Once in a while he was soft-spoken, but not often.

The Lip talked all of the time. He was around baseball a long time. He played with Babe Ruth. He was with the Gashouse Gang in St. Louis. Then he managed Willie Mays with the Giants. He was in baseball for more than 50 years. He didn't get into the Hall of Fame until after he passed on. I bet he would have made a good speech. His grandson was there, and Laraine Day was there. And I was there. I was pretty proud to be part of the Cubs organization when Leo was the manager. He gave me the opportunity to show my talent.

14

The Catcher: A Pitcher's Best Friend

A pitcher and his catcher should be on the same wavelength. The catcher needs to understand the pitcher's repertoire, his strengths and weaknesses. In an ideal working relationship between a pitcher and a catcher, they should be like brothers. I was lucky to have a long-term, close working relationship with Randy Hundley when I was with the Cubs.

The rule of thumb, in my mind, and I believe it to this day, is that the pitcher should sit by the catcher in the dugout between innings so they can talk and communicate about the hitters and what is happening in the game.

The catcher sees the reaction to all of your pitches. He can pretty much tell you which of your pitches are working and which ones aren't. Sometimes when I am watching a baseball game, I see the catcher sitting at one end of the dugout and the pitcher sitting at the other end. The catcher is your closest friend on the field. You ought to have almost as close a rapport with your catcher as you do with your wife. On game day, he's your buddy. On game day, you sit beside him. He tells you how batters are reacting.

The important part of a sinker is the last four or five inches, how it moves. The catcher tells you if the ball is moving away or down, if it has a jump to it, or not. He tells you if your slider has bite. He tells you if your rotation is good on the curveball. If you are sitting on the other end of the dugout, he's got to shout, "Hey, your curveball is working, stay with it!" No—he should be sitting next to you, telling you. I wanted that constant communication during a game.

Prior to the game, you go over all of the hitters with your catcher, but there should be a team meeting with the infielders and outfielders, as well. You go over how you are going to start out each hitter and try to refresh your memory about each one of them. Once the game starts, the catcher ought to know the first three hitters due up each inning. He's your right-hand man.

It helps if you are really friends with the catcher, too. When you're playing cards, you might go over what happened with a team. Now you have a road trip and play them again. Before opening night of a series, it's good to sit and talk with the catcher. That's something I always did, and I think is still done. I think Randy and I had a special rapport. It developed over time.

If you are going to shake off the catcher, he should know why. If you are going to shake him off, you should have a reason. You don't just run through all of the signals for the heck of it. There should be thought behind why the catcher called a pitch, and there should be thought behind why you might not want to throw that pitch at that moment.

Randy and I worked together from 1966 to 1973. It was the best relationship I had with a catcher, but it was also the longest. When I was with the Texas Rangers, I had a good rapport with Jim Sundberg. It was a little tougher when he was a rookie, but he got along with the veterans well after the first year, and he learned what he needed to do with us.

Catchers can help pitchers adjust to changing circumstances within a game. If you get a four- or five-run lead, the other team should be more aggressive trying to catch up. But some managers want their guys to work you for walks. A pitcher's concentration can wander, thinking, *Oh, man, we've got a four-run lead.* The game's not over yet. You've still got to go right after the hitters. The catcher should call the game that way. You want to keep doing what you have been doing to get the lead. Just by flashing hand signals or a nod, the catcher can help guide you. You may have the batter 0–2, and it might be the time to take a chance on a slider to strike him out. The catcher shouldn't be back there just calling the fastball.

When I first threw to Randy, I was coming out of the bullpen. There were certain times I might have had overpowering pitches because I had a lot of rest between appearances. Then as a starter I had more of a regular rhythm. Randy would always come out to the bullpen to catch me warming up before a game. The rule of thumb is for the catcher who is playing to catch the starter for the last four or five minutes of his warm-up. Before that it might be the backup. The starting catcher will go to the bullpen in all of his equipment to catch maybe 10 pitches. You run through your stuff—fastball, curveball, slider, and changeup. Then the starter gives the ball back to the bullpen catcher and goes back to the bench. Catchers have enough wear and tear on their bodies without long warm-up sessions, but they need a taste for how you are throwing that night.

Carlton Fisk and I had a good rapport when I was with the Red Sox. He was always a guy who wanted to take charge. There are reasons for a catcher to come out to the mound to talk to the pitcher. The catcher wants to get the feel of how you want to approach the guy coming to the plate. He wants to know what you are thinking your first, second, and third pitches might be. He might review the circumstances on the bases if there are bases loaded and two outs, and he'll say, "We'll come right at them." Or he'll say, "He's a first-ball fastball hitter." He might want to remind you that the batter is a breaking-ball hitter, so why don't we try coming in on his hands. Other times, the catcher might think the situation has you thinking negative, and he wants to guard against that.

Fisk liked to come out to the mound more often than other catchers. I never disliked his coming out there. He was coming out to be helpful. But he might come out five, six times a game. You might get the first three guys out, one, two, three in the first inning, then give up a walk and a double. Out he comes. He would say something like, "You've got a left-handed hitter looking for a ball down and in, so you don't want to go down and in." He was reminding you of what pitch not to throw.

Fisk probably did that more than anybody. As a veteran pitcher who had some years under my belt, I pretty much said to myself, *Hey, I've got to stay away from that.* I may or may not have known what Fisk was going to tell me, but it didn't do anybody any harm that he said it. Sometimes catchers might set up the glove outside, and you throw the ball over the plate and it gets whacked, that's your mistake. That's where control is so important. Location, location, location. Young guys who are predominantly throwers are always in trouble. Batters hit good pitches, but they hit mistakes better.

I worked with a lot of catchers. Pat Corrales and I worked together in the minors when I was still with the Phillies. Bill Plummer, J.C. Martin, and Jack Hiatt were some of the others. Different catchers react to different pitching experiences in different ways. If I hang a slider early and a guy on the other team smashes it for a double, the catcher might not say anything, but he might not want to call it again. Maybe that pitch isn't working that day, but maybe it was just that one time. I might say to a catcher, "Hey, stick with me, I'm going to throw it again. I want to keep that pitch in my rotation."

I don't think I ever yelled at a catcher on the mound during my major-league career. Once in a while I had a catcher go, "Why in hell did you shake me off?"

It's not as if pitchers don't make errors in judgment. I was with Texas, and we were playing the Baltimore Orioles. It was a good pitching matchup, too, with them throwing Hall of Famer Jim Palmer.

Earl Weaver was managing the Orioles, and he had the lineup stacked with left-handed hitters trying to get me. The guys were there for just that reason that day. In the eighth inning John Lowenstein came to the plate. He was a dangerous hitter, a good ballplayer. He fouled off the first pitch. I got ahead in the count. He took a pitch, and then he started fouling off everything. I must have thrown nine pitches to him. Jim Sundberg was calling all sliders. The count was 2–2. Lowenstein fouled off a slider. He fouled off another slider. Finally, I shook off Sunny. I wanted to throw a fastball. He called for a slider, and I shook him off again. He put down three fingers for a slider again. I threw a fastball, and Lowenstein got a base hit between first and second.

Right after the hit, Sundberg goes, "God damn it! Throw the pitch I call." He didn't really yell too loudly. He just walked out in front of the plate. I said, "That's okay, it's my ass." On the bench he reminded me of it again.

I retired the next guy. I got three outs the next inning, and we won.

Baseball is a quick-thinking game. It's reaction. Lowenstein had fouled off all of those sliders, so I thought I would throw something else. If had thrown another slider he might have just fouled that one off, too. So that's why I wanted to throw the little bastard a fastball. Only he was ready for it. The hitter out-thinks the pitcher, too. The rule of thumb is that if the batter is fouling off a lot of pitches, you throw him fastballs. Now I gave up that base hit, so I have to think, *Bad, bad, bad.* A lot of times hitters set you up for that pitch. Maybe that was a bad pitch in the arsenal I was throwing that day. I could have pitched a no-hitter, but who knows? I got close.

I probably had the most fun on the mound when I was throwing fastballs and sliders, when guys were not picking up the rotation of the ball and I had them thinking. I had a ballgame once that someone was charting, and they told me that the batters did not hit a ball in play for the first 50 pitches I threw. The first 50 pitches! I have had games where I felt crappy in warm-ups and then threw a great ballgame. You hear about guys who were sick when they came to the park and they pitched a great game. I think a lot of it is adrenaline.

When I was in the majors, I kept a book on the hitters. Cal McLish got me started on it, and Joe Becker thought it was a good thing, too. I put things in about the rookies I had never seen before. Dave Kingman, Bobby Tolan, when they came up I sat on the bench and watched them. Those guys could hit. I had to know where best to pitch them. Probably since the 1980s everything went to video. Everybody was taped, and pitchers could watch every at-bat from an opponent over and over again. Now it's on DVD. They burn those games within 10 minutes. Or they do it between innings. I just kept my observations in a notebook. After a while, I limited it to a few guys on each team that gave me trouble, guys like Willie McCovey or Roberto Clemente. Sometimes I faced a hitter for the first time, reared back, and the ball took off for a double. I went, "Damn!"

Since that movie *Bull Durham* came out with Kevin Costner playing the catcher and they had that hilarious scene where everyone is on the mound discussing what to get their teammate for a wedding present—the candlesticks scene—people ask me if we used to joke around out there, too. At Wrigley Field, I had Randy Hundley come out to the mound and go, "Man, check out the blonde walking down the third row." I said, "Come on, be serious, think about the game." He said, "I am serious. Check her out."

The year Jim Sundberg was a rookie, I wanted to talk to the umpire. I was not happy with the ump's strike zone. I yelled to Jim to come out to the mound, and I walked to the front of the mound. Meanwhile, the umpire went out to brush off the plate and bent over, so we were closer than 60'6". I lowered my voice, not yelling, and I said, "Hey, Ray, I need that pitch." The umpire turned around and said, "My name is not Ray." I said, "Yes, it's Ray Charles, but it could be Stevie Wonder if you want it to be." He started laughing. Sunny started laughing. We're all laughing out there near the mound.

I could have been sent to the showers for that, but I knew the umpire pretty well. I just wanted to get my message across that I thought the last pitch was a strike. There's a certain time and a certain way you can get on the umpire without getting tossed. I made sure I knew the umpires' names. I didn't want to just yell, "Hey, blue."

The catcher might be there whispering to the umpire, too, without turning his head, so he doesn't show the guy up. He might say, "That was a strike." But he would say it pretty softly and not make a big production of it. I hoped that it would get the umpire thinking, and maybe in the eighth inning when I needed that pitch, I would get the call. The game is a game within itself.

The mound was my office at the ballpark, and I didn't do too much fooling around out there. Even when I goofed off a little bit by making that joke with the umpire, it was about taking care of business. I was no standup comedian. I wanted every advantage I could get over the hitters who wanted to score on me, send me to the clubhouse, and put me out of work. And I would do everything I could think of to get them out and send them back to their own dugout.

15

Six Straight 20-Win Seasons and the Cy Young

By 1972, I had won 20 or more games six straight years for the Cubs. My record was: 20-13, 20-15, 21-15, 22-16, 24-13, and 20-12. I led the league in wins in 1971 with the 24 victories and won the Cy Young Award as the best pitcher in the National League.

We had the same core of excellent players, but the Cubs could not capture the pennant. Second place in 1969 with a 92-70 record was our signature season. During the 1969 season, I got the first of several tattoos. I went to a well-known tattoo shop on Belmont Avenue in Chicago on a whim and had a tattoo engraved high on my left arm. It was not the type of bawdy thing a sailor would get. Mine read, "Trust in God." The tattoo was, for me, something I wanted to do. It is so high on my arm that even when I wear a short-sleeved shirt people can't see it. Only if I have my shirt off can people read it.

In 1970 we were second again at 84-78. Near the end of the season, my mom became very ill. She had been watching the *Game of the Week* on television in mid-September, and her bladder collapsed. She didn't tell anyone right away, instead waiting until my father got home from work. Then he rushed her to the hospital. My dad called me with a shaking voice and told me that I was going to lose my mother. She was in the hospital and failing fast. I told Leo what was happening, and he told me to go right home.

When I arrived in Chatham, my mother was in intensive care. She had lost a lot of weight, so she had been sicker than she let on for a long time. She was so heavily sedated by the doctors that she barely recognized me. She knew she was dying and said, "I've lived a full life and I am happy. I'm going to see Christ." She also urged me to get back to the team as soon as possible. My mom died on Tuesday, September 15, 1970. It was her anniversary with my dad. The funeral was two days later, and my father broke down. It was the only time I saw my dad cry. I shed tears, too.

When I rejoined the team in Montreal the day after my mother's funeral, I told Leo that I wanted to pitch. I wanted to do something to honor my mother's memory. I did not pitch as well as I had hoped. I really was distracted. But I won the game, and it was my 20th victory of the season. That win was for my mother.

In 1971 we finished third at 83–79. I had a money dispute over my contract before the season. I asked for $100,000, which I knew some of the other top National League pitchers were getting, but Cubs general manager John Holland wouldn't give it to me. I signed for $92,500, and then I beat Bob Gibson and the Cardinals on Opening Day. I wanted to prove that I was in the same class as Gibson and Juan Marichal and Tom Seaver. I wanted to prove it to the Cubs, and I told the sportswriters covering the team that very thing. "The 20-win seasons are enough to me, but they're not to Mr. Holland," I said. I won my 20th game in 1971 on August 20. I had a lot of starts left. I was notified on November 3 that I had won the Cy Young Award, and I knew I wasn't going to have trouble getting $100,000 from the Cubs for the next season. I did indeed sign a two-year contract for $250,000.

Nice things that kept happening to me caught me by surprise. Apparently I was a big enough baseball star to inspire young people in Canada, and the National Film Board of Canada made a 60-minute documentary about my life.

In 1972 the Cubs gave it another run, placing second at 85–70. At the start of the season, Leo had gone out of his way to be friendly with players, to make amends with veterans he had alienated, but by mid-July he was gone, stepping down on his own, and Whitey Lockman was the manager. But we were 10 games out of first. We just couldn't get over the hump. There was always at least one team in our division that was better than we were. That season I had written down some goals for myself and the team. I put them in an envelope and taped it to my locker. We came pretty close. I won 20 games again, and the team played better than it had in a while.

Once I started putting together those 20-win seasons, Durocher just kind of let me take care of myself. Once in a while he would throw in an extra start on short rest if he needed me. That's if we were in a big series and had a chance to make a move in the standings.

We were close, but we never could get that first-place finish, and it seemed as if Leo was frustrated. He took it out on the players, maybe criticizing a little bit heavier. Milt Pappas joined the team. He was a good pitcher and a veteran who had been around. He pitched a no-hitter in 1972 and came within one walk of a perfect game. One day Leo said, "This is an open locker room. If you have something to say, I want to hear the input." Well, Milt got up and said something critical. What he didn't know was that Leo would say stuff like that all of the time, but he didn't really mean it. It was not a freedom-of-speech locker room. Milt told Leo that he had to ease up on the ridicule of young players. But Leo didn't want to hear any criticism, and he held that against Pappas.

I was charting Pappas's no-hitter. The ball that went for the walk should have been called a strike. It was close enough. It was right there. The batter took it. It would have been a perfect game.

Joe Pepitone joined the Cubs. He was a good hitter, but he was a colorful guy. He had lived it up in New York and was going to enjoy the night life in Chicago. Leo picked on Pepitone. "I saved your career," he said. "I got this and this debt paid off." He jumped on people about little things. Durocher liked Glenn Beckert. Glenn was hitting about .340 at the time, and Ron Santo was hitting about .260. He had been in a slump. Durocher jumped on Santo. He goes to Ron, "Why don't you be like your roommate. He comes out for extra batting practice all of the time." Santo was in a bad mood. He said, "I'm struggling. Don't get on me. I'm gonna break out of this slump." It almost came out as a warning. But Durocher didn't make Santo feel better, he made him madder.

Durocher made a big mistake. The year before, the team had given a day to Billy Williams. That was the day when Billy clobbered Bob Gibson in the doubleheader. Durocher started ragging on Ron. He accused Ronnie of demanding a day because he couldn't get more money out of management in his contract and he wanted to make it up with presents. Ronnie got furious. He said, "What the hell are you talking about? I didn't ask for a day." Durocher kept it up, and Ronnie jumped out of his chair and was going to choke Leo.

The guys held Ronnie back, but Kenny Holtzman, who didn't get along with Leo by then, yelled, "Let him go! Let him go!" He wanted to see Ronnie strangle Leo. Oh man, it was incredible. And then right there Leo said he was quitting. It got to be a few minutes to game time, and there was no Leo. We were all still in the locker room. We didn't warm up. We didn't take infield practice. The starting pitcher hadn't warmed up. John Holland, the general manager came down, and the game was delayed about 20 minutes.

The game got played, and afterward Durocher went to P.K. Wrigley and said he needed things straightened out in the clubhouse. An article came out in the paper the next day that said Leo wasn't going anywhere. Mr. Wrigley said, "We're keeping Leo, and everybody else is going. Nobody can think they are that important. We are trading the team." Mr. Wrigley supported Leo as manager no matter what.

This was a team that had good chemistry with guys who are still friends 40 years later. It may have seemed to someone else that Leo was the problem, and that since he hadn't won yet, it was time for him to go. I still have to think that near-fight in the locker room was the prelude to Leo's departure the next season. Maybe he wanted to go out on his own terms so it wouldn't look as if he had been pushed, and not leave in the middle of a mutiny.

There were differences when Whitey became manager. Leo used to leave me in to work out of jams, especially in close games. But when Whitey took over in the later innings if it was 1–1 or 2–2, I was gone. I had been pitching more than 300 innings, and I pitched 271 innings that year. Whitey took me out of games earlier. Leo had confidence in me. The team was starting to change. The Cubs bought players. The team had less power in the lineup. The team was really broken up.

After winning 20 games every season, believe me, I was not used to losing. Finishing 14–16 appalled me. I came into the season hoping I could set a record for winning 20 games in a season seven straight years. Whitey just didn't seem to have the needed confidence in me. At one point I just got fed up with what was going on, not pitching as well as I wanted to, Whitey pulling me out. We were playing against the Atlanta Braves at Wrigley Field, and Hank Aaron was going for what was probably his 700th career home run.

It was around the fifth inning, and I gave up a walk. Whitey chews me out for the walk and two hitters later he replaces me with a relief pitcher. The Braves got some hits off of him and some runs. The bat racks were right in front of the dugout. I grabbed some bats and heaved them onto the field. When the bats hit the grass, they skidded and almost went past the umpire. I got ejected from the game.

I had to walk from the dugout down the left-field line to the clubhouse. Ron Santo asks me, "Fergie, are you out of here?" And I said, "Yes!" I just wanted to blow off some steam. Well, the next day John Holland came to me and said he wanted me to see a therapist. He thought I was going to have a breakdown because he had never seen me get frustrated like that. A lot of things were going on. Kathy had had a miscarriage. And I was pissed off at the manager. Then they started saying I had a sore arm. I had had some cortisone shots in spring training, but that was it. My arm was fine. I did not have tendonitis. I was throwing okay. I just was not getting good results. What really bothered me was that the Cubs started to say that I had a bad arm. That was a bunch of crap.

I still believe if we had won in 1969, we would have won again in 1970. The only weakness we had was the bullpen. If John Holland could have brought in some relievers, we would have done it. One thing I think that group of players accomplished was to change the way Cubs fans rooted for the team. The team had been bad for so long. We created excitement. We had winning records. We had a team in contention. We drew more than 1.6 million people at a time when that was very good. We started things off for the Cubs. In a way it was the beginning of modern Cubs popularity. We had popular guys like Ernie Banks, Billy Williams, Ron Santo, and me. Glenn Beckert and Don Kessinger were in the mix. Randy Hundley. We jump-started the club.

We became winners. We beat up on a lot of other teams that had been beating up on the Cubs. The Cardinals couldn't beat us the way they had. The Dodgers couldn't beat us the way they had been. We let them all know that we weren't going to roll over.

Things started to change. Ernie Banks retired after the 1971 season, so he was the first one in our group to give up the game. Kenny Holtzman was traded to Oakland in a deal that brought Rick Monday to Chicago in 1972. After my six straight 20-game-win seasons, I had an off-year in 1973, not even close to what I had been producing. What shocked me was how quickly everybody seemed to give up on me. It was like none of those other years had counted. Suddenly, it was as if I was all washed up.

I asked John Holland what he was going to do to bring in other guys to improve the team. I had a bad year in 1973, and all of a sudden I was reading in the newspaper how "Jenkins has a bad arm." I wasn't injured.

When the season ended, I returned to Canada. I was on a fishing trip in Ontario, and when I got back to the house, my wife told me to call the Cubs. I reached Blake Cullen, the traveling secretary, and he told me I had been traded to the Texas Rangers for two players. I didn't know anything about the Texas Rangers. They were in the American League, and I had been in the National League my entire career. I didn't know any of the players. I had no connections there except I knew that Billy Martin was the manager.

I was upset because I was literally waved out of the National League. Yes, it was a trade, but you would have thought one of the teams in the league that had been watching me over the years would want me. I asked Blake Cullen why the Cubs traded me out of the National League. He just said that they got two young infielders.

I had grown up with the Phillies, and they traded me. I had terrific success with the Cubs, and they traded me. I had been a Cub in my allegiance and in my head. I always thought of myself as a National League player. Going to the American League, I wasn't even going to bat. They had the designated hitter by then.

It took me some time to digest the trade. It took time for the news to really sink into my brain, *Hey, you've been traded.*

If I was going to be traded, I wanted to stay in the National League. If I was going to be traded, I wanted to go to a contending team. This trade accomplished neither of those things. But I wasn't ready to retire. I still felt I had a lot of pitching to do, and I wanted to prove to the Cubs that they had made a mistake getting rid of me. It would have been easier to do that if I was still in the National League and I pitched against the Cubs all of the time. I would just have to show them by pitching well in the American League.

I was really worried about everybody giving me a bad rap, saying I had a sore arm. When I got to spring training with the Rangers, the first thing I did was go talk to Billy Martin and assure him my arm was fine and to just give me the ball and I would win for him.

16

Texas

When I joined the Texas Rangers for spring training in 1974, I was on a mission to show that I belonged and that I could still be a 20-game winner.

I went back to Canada after the 1973 season, but I didn't realize just how energetically the Cubs were shopping me around. There was a story in *The Sporting News* that had this headline: "Cubs on Fergie: 'Make Us An Offer.'" I guess the Cubs were trying pretty hard to get rid of me.

In that story, John Holland said, "There are no untouchables." It was unusual enough that the Cubs didn't flat out deny they were trying to trade me. That was their normal procedure. They never talked about trades until they happened. They just seemed to be so determined. One season of 14–16 had eliminated all of the good will I built up with six 20-win seasons. The fans booed me for the only time that summer, and at one point I asked my wife to stay away from Wrigley Field and to keep the kids at home instead of coming to watch me play. At that point in my career, I had won 149 games, 147 of them for the Cubs.

The Cubs didn't wait long after the interleague trading period opened, either, shipping me to Texas for Vic Harris and Bill Madlock. Obviously, with Madlock, they got a pretty good hitter. Madlock became a batting champion.

Reporters tracked me down in Canada at the time, and I said, "There was no animosity between me and the Cubs. It was just time for me to leave. I asked for only one special favor. I asked Holland if he would trade me to a team as close to my home as possible. He gave me a funny look, and I should have known he would send me as far away as possible."

Part of me still didn't really believe that I would be traded away from the Cubs, and I never thought for a minute that I would be traded out of the National League. That caught me more by surprise than anything.

Spring training was in Florida. The Rangers' headquarters were in Pompano Beach. We stayed in a bungalow-type hotel right on the beach called the Surf Riders Club. We were very close to Fort Lauderdale, and that was one of the biggest gathering places of college students for spring break. There were a lot of girls coming down for spring break, but I am not really a beach person. I walked around a lot, but I don't need a tan.

Joe Namath had a nightclub in Fort Lauderdale called "Broadway Joe's," but we weren't allowed to go in. We were told that it was Mafia connected, that undesirables hung out there. So the baseball commissioner's office told the teams that trained in the area not to go in and not to fraternize with the customers from Broadway Joe's. With that lockout and not liking the beach much, there wasn't much to do in Pompano Beach. There were a couple of decent restaurants, but that was it.

This was a completely fresh start for me. I was with a new team, in a new league, with a new manager, new management, and new teammates. I was coming off a losing season, and I didn't know how I would be viewed. Very early on I became friendly with Jim Bibby, another pitcher. He had come over from the Cardinals during the previous season. We struck up a conversation, and he asked if I wanted to room with him. So we did and became very good friends. Jim was about 6'6", and even though they said he weighed 240, I am sure he was a lot bigger. I called him "Giant" as a nickname. He was a big dude, and we seemed to be on the same wavelength.

The Rangers had been very active in the trade market, and they had a lot of new guys who had come in from maybe a half-dozen organizations. Alex Johnson, whom I had known in the Phillies' organization, was there, as were Steve Hargan, Reggie Cleveland, and Toby Harrah. There were some good young players, like our catcher Jim Sundberg,

Mike Hargrove, Lenny Randle, Pete Broberg, and Don Stanhouse. Jeff Burroughs was a good power hitter. It was kind of a United Nations, with guys from different teams trying to blend in.

Out of the whole 40-man roster, I knew about three people when I came over to the Rangers. Half the guys, I didn't even know their names. We would see each other at breakfast and say, "Hey, what's going on?" I didn't know any of the coaches, either. It was a pretty strange spring for me.

We opened the season against Oakland, in Texas, and I went with my usual plan and wore a long-sleeved shirt. I kept it up later, too, even when it was 90 degrees. Jim Bibby pitched the first game. Catfish Hunter, who became a Hall of Famer, beat us 7-2.

I started the second game. It felt like we had a nice crowd on a nice day, although there were only about 17,000 people there. The opposing pitcher for the A's was my old friend, Kenny Holtzman. The second batter in their lineup was another old friend, Bert Campaneris, and he got a single in the fourth. Campaneris, who was one of the best base runners of his time, tried to steal second, and we erased him.

And that was it until I walked Manny Trillo in the ninth. I pitched a one-hitter and pitched to only 28 men, one over the minimum, in my first game as a Texas Ranger. I struck out 10, and we won 2-0. Our lineup had Tom Grieve as the designated hitter, which pretty much had just been adopted; Jim Fregosi at first base; Dave Nelson at second; Toby Harrah at short; Larry Brown at third; and Sunny was the catcher. The outfielders were Alex Johnson, Burroughs, and Joe Lovitto. Poor Joe had a tumor in his stomach and died from cancer in 2001. He was a very fast runner who was always held back by injuries. We left a lot of men on base because we had our share of hits. Kenny didn't get out of the fifth inning that day.

I made a good first impression with Texas. I was popping the ball pretty well. I only walked one batter. That performance got me off on the right foot with the whole organization, including the fans. I showed them right away that I could win. The team started off pretty well, but went into a tailspin. I pitched pretty well, but I went back and forth. I won and I lost. I was 9-9 at one point, but then I won 14 of my next 16 decisions.

I had never lived anyplace like Texas, but I loved it. That was ranching country. I had my 10-gallon hats. Texas was also a very good place to fish. I did a lot of fishing in Texas. That was my main way to relax. A lot of the other guys liked to fish, too. Jim Kern, Doyle Alexander, a bunch of the guys would pile onto a boat, and we'd go out on a lake to kill time. The bass were running. It was hot, though. There were plenty of days in the summer when it was 100 degrees.

I got into trouble once when I went fishing on a day that I was scheduled to pitch. It was a great fishing day, and I was catching a lot of big fish. I left the lake too late and got caught in traffic. I was supposed to be at the ballpark at 4:00 PM and didn't make it until 6:00 PM. They were running around going, "Where's Jenkins?" In the players' parking area, there was a guard, and I pulled up, jumped out of the car, with the boat still in tow, tossed him the keys, and yelled, "Park it for me!"

There was no way I could sneak into the clubhouse. Everyone was saying, "Where have you been?" I didn't lie about it. I didn't use one of those the-dog-ate-my-homework excuses. I just said, "I've been catching fish." I had about 60 minutes to get ready for the game. Not ideal. A couple of the coaches came over to my locker, which wasn't any surprise, either.

Billy Martin was just as tough as Leo Durocher. He was a no-nonsense manager, too. He wanted you to win, and he wanted you to perform. Like Leo, he hated excuses. No alibis. If you pitched well, fine. But if you went out there and someone else made an error and you lost, he didn't want you to blame the other person. Just suck it up. He didn't like excuses, and he didn't like guys to whine on the bench. He wanted you to play hard, do the right thing, and enjoy winning. Then go out there the next day and do it again. That's what he believed in.

Martin wanted me in his office. I walked in and said, "What's up?" As if I didn't know. He looked at his watch. He asked me, "Are you going to be all right?" I said, "I'm fine. I'm okay." I went through my regimen of hanging up my clothes and putting on my uniform and seeing the trainer. I did my thing. I lathered more heat stuff on my arm than I usually did. You might say there was a little bit of pressure on me to pitch well that night. It would not have been good to get lit up for seven runs early.

I was lucky. I pitched a great game, and we beat the Angels. I was a winner and did a good job. If I had pitched poorly because I was breaking the rules, Martin would have creamed me. He would have said something for sure. This is what you call being a clutch pitcher.

The 1974 season turned into a great year for me. I finished 25-12. I led the American League in wins and won more games that season than in any other. The Rangers had moved to Texas for the 1972 season, so they were pretty new in Arlington, too. The franchise had been the Washington Senators, but the team moved west because the population was growing in the Dallas area. They didn't really have a stadium to play in yet. The park was originally called Turnpike Stadium, but they changed the name to Arlington Stadium before they built the new Ballpark at Arlington in the 1990s.

The ballpark was small, and it had a wind factor. The wind made the field a good hitter's park. The place seemed like it was almost all bleachers. It was not double-decked. It was just one tier all of the way up, 30, 50 rows—that's the way the grandstand was. The wind swirled. It blew out to right field early in a night game, and it blew out to left later in the game. You had to use your head and watch the flag, or you would be giving up home runs all of the time.

For the most part, I coped with the heat, but I had to hydrate well. I drank a lot of water. I put ice on my wrists and my elbow to keep myself cool. There were two times when we had a sudden infestation of insects swarming us on the field to the point where it drove us nuts. One time it was grasshoppers. The other time it was crickets. They were all over the field. They descended on the game by the millions. They started by swarming around the lights, then came onto the field. I was not pitching either of those days, but it was unbelievable to see. It was like the Bible with locusts. Both times the games were stopped. There were so many grasshoppers and crickets that the grounds crew had to shovel them off the field.

One thing that was different for me in Texas was the amount of firepower the lineup had. I remember saying early in the season I had never pitched in back-to-back games where my team had scored at least 10 runs.

When I got to the Rangers, they were still using pitcher David Clyde, trying to make him a superstar hero for the fans because he was local and had a lot of talent. Clyde was a high school phenom at age 18, and the Rangers drafted him and threw him right into the majors. The idea was to capitalize on his popularity and make money off his name with big crowds. Instead, the team ruined him. Clyde went 4-8 as a rookie, and his second year, 1974, when I came to Texas, he went 3-9.

It's difficult to tell what would have happened if David had gone to the minors as he should have, worked on developing into a pitcher instead of just a raw, talented fastball thrower. He had the ability. He just didn't have any luck. He pitched some decent games, but he couldn't win them. He might have had a normal career. Instead, he was out of the majors in five years with a lifetime record of 18-33. It was a shame. The team just had no patience to nurture him along. They might have ended up with a star for 10 years instead of a shooting star for a game or two. You would like to think that every team in the majors learned from that and they won't ever rush a high schooler into the role of being a savior just weeks after graduation.

In 1974, the season I won 25 games, I should have had 26 wins. The officials gave the team a win, as a forfeit, instead of me.

We were playing the Cleveland Indians in Texas. Milt Wilcox was pitching for Cleveland. It was about the third inning, and we had Lenny Randle at bat. Lenny had been a good football player at Arizona State. Wilcox threw a good pitch, and Lenny bunted it down the first-base line. Wilcox ran over to cover first, and Randle ran right over him. A fight started, and we had a 20-minute brawl, knocking heads. A lot of people make fun of baseball fights, but these were real fights.

The cops came out on the field. Peace prevailed. Lenny got ejected and so did Milt Wilcox. The game resumed, and I don't even remember which team won. But soon after that we traveled to Cleveland. I was the scheduled Texas pitcher in the first game, and it was 10¢ beer night. There were a lot of photographers and cameramen and press because this was the first time we played since the big brawl.

A few innings into the game, Leron Lee hit a line drive off my leg. That play was my closest call on the mound. He knocked me over. The trainer came out and looked at me, and when I stayed in the game, the fans gave me a standing ovation. I was winning the game and, in-between innings, icing my leg in the dugout. A few more runs scored, and I was leading 5-2 in the sixth inning. An Indians player creamed a pitch for a double, and when I ran over to back up Jim Fregosi at third base, he accidentally stepped on my leg.

That gave me a big gash, and blood poured through my sock. During the timeout, two guys sitting in the outfield mooned the crowd. We had a streaker on the field. That's the kind of stuff that happens on 10¢ beer night. The two guys who mooned the crowd ran onto the field. A woman wearing a tank top lifted the top. Everybody was drinking tons of beer, and they were nuts. Then some fans started throwing stuff on the field. Somebody in the upper deck threw a chair.

I had been hit by a line drive and spiked, but I was winning the game 5-2. After two injuries, we decided that was enough for me, and it was time to bring in someone from the bullpen. The cut from Lenny's spikes was so bad I had to be taken to the hospital. I got taken to the emergency room and was put on a gurney while I was still in uniform.

While waiting, the doors opened, and medical workers from an ambulance burst in with two customers. One had a big gash on his face, and the other guy seemed to be bleeding all over. They told me there was a riot going on at Municipal Stadium. I said, "Whoa, what do you mean?" I was sitting there in my stinking, sweaty Texas Rangers uniform bleeding, and I'd just left the stadium.

One guy said, "They're throwing chairs from the upper deck! They're going crazy! They're rioting!" In the next 15 minutes, two more ambulances pulled up. Then some more patients came in who were all cut up. I demanded to make a phone call. I telephoned the visitors locker room and reached clubhouse man Bill Sheraton. We called him "the Hotel Man" because his last name was Sheraton. I asked him what the hell was going on.

He said, "Fergie, all the players are locked in the clubhouse. They're having a riot in the stadium. What you need to do is catch a cab or get somebody to take you back to the hotel and change your clothes there. You can't get back in the clubhouse. They've locked all the players in." I asked, "What happened with the game?"

Sheraton told me the umpires called the game off. "They forfeited," he said. "The team got the win."

I said, "What do you mean the team got the win? I was winning the ballgame!" The next day in the paper the final score was 9–0, a forfeit score. There was also a picture with fans on the field chasing after Jeff Burroughs as if they wanted to fight with him. That wouldn't have been too smart. Billy Martin and the coaches were running out there to protect him. The whole thing was incredible. But I should have been the pitcher of record.

I was kind of an overnight star in Texas, winning 25 games my first year with the team and winning the Comeback Player of the Year award. The second season did not go as smoothly. I finished 17–18. The team never caught fire, and we finished 79–83. The owners had hoped for more. Still, I had made myself pretty popular in Texas pretty quickly. Guys don't just show up out of the blue and win 25 games.

I always had a great time in Texas. The fans were nice to me. Management was good to me. I pitched well there. And, as it turned out years later, the organization remembered me. In 2004 I received a very unexpected phone call from the Rangers. They said, "Fergie, you've been elected to the Texas Rangers Hall of Fame." Yes, they meant the Rangers baseball Hall of Fame, not the Texas Rangers law enforcement Hall of Fame, though they do have one where they honor the lawmen who caught a bunch of bad guys.

The player I was inducted with was Buddy Bell, and I thought that was great because we had been teammates. The ceremony was neat. The team held the event at the ballpark at a game, and the building was sold out. When you are chosen for the Rangers Hall of Fame, they make up a special bronze plaque that you get to keep. I swear that thing weighed 100 pounds. It's huge and heavy.

One thing that was brought up when I was chosen for the Rangers Hall of Fame was my 25-win season in 1974. Although the Rangers had also had Nolan Ryan on the roster, some of the newspapers argued that my year was the best season a Rangers' pitcher ever had. I pitched 328⅓ innings that summer, and my earned-run average was 2.82.

For the ceremony at the game, the plaque was already on a pedestal, but covered by a cloth. When they unveiled it, this guy's job was to pick it up and stand by me and my family. I have a picture of this little guy lifting it and almost falling over. After the ceremony, they shipped the plaque to my home in a box, and I have it in the family room next to my Cy Young Award.

The people in Chicago don't realize the ties I have to Texas. I go there for special events a lot. Part of me is definitely a Ranger. I didn't have quite the connection with the Red Sox, but I am part of the Boston Red Sox Alumni. I get a newsletter about all the former players. I don't have much of a relationship with the Phillies. I barely pitched for them early in my career, and that seems like a long time ago. Gene Dziadura, just as he was in the beginning, is my closest tie to the Phillies.

But after my second year with the Texas Rangers, I was traded to the Boston Red Sox for Juan Beniquez, Steve Barr, and a pitcher to be named later who turned out to be Craig Skok. I was on my way to the defending American League champions for the start of the 1976 season. I was headed north, and I was headed to a winner. I didn't realize that some very strange times lay ahead.

17

Boston

Bernie Carbo was a character. The Red Sox had a lot of characters on the team. I probably had more fun with the Red Sox off the field than anywhere else I played.

Although Carlton Fisk's home run in the 1975 World Series against the Reds gets most of the attention, Bernie's three-run homer before that was just as important and kept the Red Sox alive.

Some older movie fans might remember there was a film that featured a gorilla called Mighty Joe Young. Bernie had a stuffed white gorilla that he called Whitey Joe Young. He carried it everywhere and talked to it. It was about five feet tall. He talked to it all the time. He brought it on the plane with him—we had charters—and sat it in the seat next to him. "Tonight's going to be Bernie's night," he had the gorilla say. We were all over him about the gorilla and carrying it around in public. We kept telling him, "People will start thinking crazy things about you." But he always said, "I don't care." Whitey Joe Young.

My first year in Boston was 1976. The Sox had taken Cincinnati to the seventh game of the World Series the preceding year. I got 29 starts and finished 12–11 with a 3.27 earned-run average. I pitched okay. It was not my best year, but I did a pretty good job for the Red Sox.

The biggest problem I had in Boston was dealing with the manager, Don Zimmer. We didn't get along very well, and worse, from his standpoint, was that I hung out with all of the guys he didn't like and thought were a bad influence on the ballclub. One of my best buddies on that team was Bill Lee, the "Spaceman." Spaceman Lee was a very funny guy. He had a terrific sense of humor and was very irreverent. He was not a yes-man, the type of guy who fit into a corporate structure, or who was likely to wear a sports jacket and tie all of the time. Bill said what he thought and what he thought could be pretty blunt. The media loved Spaceman Lee. But people have to remember, he was a very good pitcher and was the key southpaw on the team.

There were five of us who shared a corner in the locker room. I was there with Bill Lee; my old friend, Rick Wise; Jim Willoughby, a relief pitcher; and Bernie Carbo. There is no doubt that Bill Lee is one of the biggest wisecrackers who ever played baseball, and that group got labeled as the rebels of the team. We all felt we should be playing more than we were at the time, and I think statistical evidence was on our side. We kind of got shunted aside, not just physically in the clubhouse, but when it came to playing time. We were frustrated, and to make up for those feelings, we goofed around a lot, cracked jokes, and blamed our circumstances on the manager.

This was the famous time period when Bill Lee called Don Zimmer "a gerbil." Our group got ourselves a different nickname—"the Buffalo Head Gang." *The Boston Globe* ran a caricature illustration of Zimmer in the newspaper and exaggerated the size of his head way out of proportion, and at the same time drew stick limbs for arms and legs. So there was Zimmer with this gigantic head. Zimmer did not think the picture was very flattering and disliked it. I cut it out of the paper and put it up in my locker. At the bottom I attached the words "Buffalo Head," even though it had no meaning.

However, my pals in the corner wanted a definition. So I quickly concocted a story about how the buffalo head in the picture reminded me of a real buffalo and how the Indians drove the buffalo over cliffs to harvest them in groups for their needs. I was just winging it. Bill Lee later said that I added in "the fact" that buffalo were the dumbest animals on earth, though I doubt that's true. That's how the buffalo-head theme got attached to Zimmer and how we became the Buffalo Head Gang.

We didn't have a lot of respect for how Zimmer was running the team. We thought he was misusing his personnel, especially us. Lee went to the bullpen, even though we needed a lefty starter. Rick and

I weren't full-time regulars in the starting rotation. Willoughby wasn't getting used.

At the same time, our little group had completely commandeered the corner of the locker room and treated it like a fraternity zone. We weren't too extreme, but a tipping point came after a *Playboy* centerfold hanging in my locker was noticed by a group of private citizens touring Fenway Park.

The reason the magazines were even at the ballpark was my trade from Texas. I had been subscribing to *Playboy* at home, but when I changed teams, I didn't have a forwarding address, so I just had all of my mail sent to Fenway Park. There was a very beautiful Jamaican girl who was the Playmate for December, and since it was my birthday month, I put it up. Other guys had their wives and kids and cats and dogs hanging there. When we went on the road, I covered the picture up with a towel so nobody walking past could see it. I don't know what happened with those visitors, but when I came back to my locker, the towel was gone and the picture was gone. Zimmer got angry about the centerfold and said he didn't want any of that in the locker room. The picture of the buffalo-head Zimmer replaced the Playmate. Some people would have said that was a bad trade.

You could tell from the way we were used and the way Zimmer felt about us that the five of us were all short-timers, that we all were going to get traded. Eventually, we were. I said, "We probably won't all be together again, but for now we are the Buffalo Head Gang."

The Buffalo Head Gang socialized together, went out after games together, played cards. We were a clique. One time we had a day off in Oakland, and in our travels on the BART train we lost Bernie. He later said he met a cab driver who gave him a smoke, marijuana. When we found him, he was high and was lying on a park bench. When we were playing cards, if Bill Lee lost a hand, he'd throw the cards down on the table, go out in the hallway, run up and down four or five times, and then take his seat at the table again.

It was a good bunch of guys. We had fun, but we worked hard. If Zimmer had just left us alone, we could have really helped the Red Sox. It's supposed to be a fun game.

After years of pitching for the Cubs and having Wrigley Field as my home ballpark, I had the opportunity to experience the Red Sox and Fenway Park the same way. They are the two most iconic baseball parks in the country, and it was pretty special to have the chance to play in both cities, where the ballparks have been part of the franchise for almost 100 years.

I think the fans were very knowledgeable in Boston. As a pitcher, you knew it was a small park, and you had to work around that, but I never had any problems. It was short down the line. We had the Green Monster looming over our shoulder with the high wall so close in left. But I had already played at Wrigley, so Fenway Park was a piece of cake. I really enjoyed pitching in Fenway. Fenway has an intimate atmosphere that everyone loves. Both Wrigley Field and Fenway Park were built in neighborhoods, right across the street from where people live.

I knew what pitches to throw. I stayed with my strength and I tried to stay away from the hitters' strengths. I gave up hits off the wall, but they didn't go out. There were hard shots off the wall that were only singles because we had either Carl Yastrzemski or Jim Rice out there. They knew how to play the wall. It was second nature to them. So they would play the carom, the ball would come off the wall into their gloves, and they would throw some guys out at second who thought they were going to be in there for doubles. Instead, they ended up either with long singles, if they turned back, or a single and an out on the same play.

Carl Yastrzemski was the left-fielder some of the time. But he also played first base and designated hitter. He was on his way to the Hall of Fame. I didn't really know him before I came to the Red Sox. He was a quiet guy. He was a powerful guy, strong, so much so that he looked like a football player. Oh, he could hit. Fred Lynn was a spray hitter. Dewey Evans was a terrific outfielder and hit with power. He was a Hall of Fame outfielder. It's hard to get into the Hall of Fame as a fielder, but he could field the ball and throw bullets from right field. He could run the bases, too. The only thing he might have lacked was power. I'll tell you, with his arm, which was like Roberto Clemente's, nobody ran on Dewey Evans. To me he was the white Roberto Clemente. He threw the ball on a line from right field to second or to third. And Jim Rice definitely belongs in the Hall of Fame.

Something the Red Sox fans and the Cubs fans had in common when I played in Boston and Chicago was that they rarely seemed to boo their own players. Everybody is entitled to have a bad game. Mostly, if I got knocked out in the fifth or sixth inning, they were understanding and would say, "You'll get them next time, Fergie," or, "We're behind you." There was a lot of encouragement. We had open parking lots for the players at both places, and the fans could cut through on the way to their own cars. If you were out there and the fans were still coming by, they would walk right past your car, shake your hand, and say, "Hey, great game."

The Cubs had not won a World Series since 1908 and had not been in the World Series since 1945. The Red Sox had not won the World Series since 1918, but they had been in the Series the year before. For that reason, I felt that the Cubs fans were hungrier to win. Then the Red Sox won the Series in 2004 and 2007. They got two. I have just always been hoping that the Cubs would win the World Series in my lifetime.

When I was traded from Texas to Boston, I was excited because I was going to a winning team. I thought it was my chance to win a championship. It was disappointing to sort of get shoved aside. Even worse, however, was suffering the most serious injury of my baseball career, an injury that I was fortunate did not end my career.

With about three-quarters of the 1976 season gone, I had started 29 games for Boston and had a 12–11 record. It seemed likely much of the rest of my season was going to be spent in the bullpen. But before that could happen, I had a serious accident on the field. We were playing against my old team, the Texas Rangers, and Lenny Randle hit a slow roller of a ground ball that was scooped up by Cecil Cooper, the Red Sox's first baseman. I was racing over to cover first, and Cooper tossed the ball to me.

As I ran over to the bag to make the play, I felt a searing pain in my right heel. I had ruptured my Achilles tendon. The pain was intense, and I knew right away that the injury was going to take a long time to heal. It felt almost as if someone had shot me in the heel.

I was taken to the hospital and had surgery. I was told that I was going to have to undergo six months of rehabilitation work. For the first time, my career was in jeopardy. No one could promise me that I would ever pitch as well again. Nobody but me. I knew I would have to work as hard as I ever had to get into shape. That was the new challenge for a pitcher who in the off-season would turn 34. Once I was healthy and ready to pitch again, as I was determined to be, I also didn't know if anyone would want me. I would have to prove once again that I could still be a regular starting pitcher in someone's rotation. If I was going to make a comeback and pitch like the Fergie of old, I could not allow any doubts to seep into my own mind.

18

The Achilles Injury

My damaged Achilles was a major injury, unlike anything else I had ever faced during my baseball career.

I returned home to Canada in the autumn of 1976 to my ranch to recuperate after leaving Boston, and everything was a struggle. I had a lot of pain. I was under doctor's orders not to do too much. I was supposed to sit around and do nothing. But that's not me, and I got bored pretty quickly. Doing nothing did not suit me at all.

When you live on a ranch or farm, something always needs doing. Animals that need care, crops that need tending, fences that need mending. There is never nothing to do, so there was always a temptation for me to do something, even if I had help from my dad or hired help.

Winter, as most people in the United States know, arrives pretty early in Ontario. On a day in late October, it was about 20 degrees when I decided that the mare in the nearby barn that was scheduled to deliver a colt might need help. I definitely thought I should look in on her. It was not that far from the main house to the barn, maybe a half mile, but I was not going to walk it on ice and snow. So I gingerly climbed into my pickup truck. The injured Achilles was on my right foot, so I couldn't really step on the gas. You might say I steered the truck more than actually drove it the few minutes it took to reach the barn.

I eased my way out of the driver's side and slowly, very slowly, started to make my way to the barn. I was maybe 15 feet from the truck when I took a bad spill. I slipped on the ice. Boom! I hit the ground, the ice, and the snow hard. I landed on my back, mostly jarring my right side. My first thought was not about the Achilles—although that was a big enough problem—but that I had broken my kneecap.

Because I was only planning to drive right up the road, I hadn't put on heavy layers of clothing. I had on long underwear and coveralls on my legs and a heavy wool shirt with a jacket over it. I had on a hunting sock that came about halfway up my calf and a hunting boot on the outside. There was some water on the ground, too, so I was getting wet. When I fell, I could hardly move. I ripped my pants and I just lay there for a while. This was the first time in my life I was lying helpless somewhere outdoors where I couldn't get up. That was my first thought, trying to stand up, but I couldn't. I couldn't get turned over at first, either. My foot and knee throbbed.

I tried to collect my thoughts. It was about 7:30 in the morning, and it was still a bit overcast. There was no one around. My wife was back at the house. I thought about yelling for help, but it didn't make any sense because no one could hear me. I was mad at myself for falling. As I lay there I could feel rock salt melting underneath me, too. The truck was probably warmer than the barn, but I was determined to get indoors in the barn. That was my goal. The barn was a little bit closer than the truck. I figured I could get in the barn door.

Of course, I had to move first and I was almost paralyzed on the ground, just stuck there. My knees wouldn't bend. I don't know whether it was the awkwardness of my foot being useless, if I was stunned from the fall, or what, but I just couldn't get up. I lay there for a long time. I kind of regrouped and set my sights on a snow bank outside the barn door, thinking if I reach the snow bank, I could raise myself up a little bit and sit there, and then make it inside the barn.

Given the temperature, the fact that I ripped my clothing, and I was wet, I could have gotten hypothermia very easily, but I wasn't thinking of hypothermia at all. I was thinking about how much pain I had in my knee. It was killing me. I dragged myself over to the snow bank and managed to sit down in the snow—or rather pull myself up to sit down. There were a lot of things running through my mind, but I knew I couldn't just stay there. I had to move myself. It was frustrating. You're used to your body listening to you and doing what you tell it to do, especially if you are an athlete. My body had its ears blocked. It wasn't responding at all.

This whole time, nobody really knew where I was or what I was doing. Heck, even the mare didn't seem like she knew anyone was there. She didn't make any noise. I couldn't really stand up from the snow bank, either. I got back down on the ground and crawled to the barn door. I pulled myself into the barn, and I think I scared her at that point. I startled the mare as she was giving birth to the colt. It was hanging halfway out of her. Inside the barn, I pulled myself to my feet and spent about 25 or 30 minutes helping the mare deliver the colt.

I was concentrating more on the mare than I was on the pain in my leg. When I came out of her stall, I opened the gate and saw some towels. I wiped the colt down a little bit and the mare did the rest. She started nuzzling it. I figured the colt was going to be okay because it was breathing and had its head up.

Then I worked my way back to the truck, hauled myself in, and spent the next five or so minutes driving back to the house. I went up the driveway and into the garage. Kathy was in the kitchen. I was all wet, and she looked at me and said, "What happened to you?"

I said, "I fell. Oh, and by the way, Sassy has a colt. Do you want to go back out and see?"

Kathy looked at me a little strangely, but I was being very manly about the whole thing and didn't tell her what had happened. I was hurting, though. My knee hurt more by the minute.

I took off my jacket, undid the clips on the coveralls, and slid them off. When I took the coveralls off, I saw I had split them. My underwear was wet. Man, that meant I had to climb the stairs to change. I started hopping up the stairs. My dad came up from the basement and said, "What's wrong, son?" I just told him I was okay and about the colt and how Kathy was going to go out and look at it and she probably could use some help.

Everything hurt so badly that it took me an hour to peel off my clothes, change into new clothes, and look myself over. There was no bruising, no blood, no visible sign of a problem with my knee. It just ached. I took some Tylenol and rested, sitting on the side of the bed. Kathy and my dad came back and said the colt was up and nursing.

If my doctor had come to the house and heard what had happened, he would have said how stupid I had been to go out on the ice. I can't imagine what the Red Sox would have said. As far as they knew, I was being extra cautious at home rehabbing my Achilles tendon. Smashing up my knee probably did not qualify as part of the regularly scheduled rehab program. I was really alarmed that I might have done some serious damage to the knee and that it would interfere with my coming back to pitch, but it got better faster than the Achilles.

This was one very long and painful off-season. I had a series of five casts on the Achilles. When they did the surgery, I got an open cast that ran up to my calf and had a drainage hole. I had 20 stitches. I have a four-inch scar. It healed pretty well, but it took a while before I could tie a work boot tight on it because my ankle was so swollen. I wear a size 12, so I went to a store and bought size 13s and wore the right boot on my right foot for a while. The last cast was removed in January of 1977 in Boston. Spring training was just around the corner.

I had to learn to walk normally again because I had been swinging my leg in a certain way because of the casts. I had to convince my brain not to swing my leg anymore. The first thing the doctors did was stimulate my right leg with machines because the muscles had atrophied. They kept moving my heel, up and down, up and down. Then they worked on my calf because that muscle was smaller. I did some exercises in a pool. The rehab was long, demanding, and painful.

Some people had said my career was in jeopardy, that I might not be able to pitch again. My goal was to get to spring training in good shape. I knew there was nothing wrong with my arm. My thought was, "I'm definitely going to do this." That was my motivation to work through the rehab. A lot of the rehab was done in Boston. In February I was walking in a regular shoe, and I walked a lot on a treadmill. It was nice and slow, and I was wearing a high-topped running shoe. The foot was killing me, but I didn't let anybody know. I just kept doing it and doing it and doing it.

Each time I worked out, my ankle got hot and swollen. I took the shoe off and iced it down. I iced it down every day and continued to do that through spring training. At Red Sox spring training, pitchers and catchers were to report in late February in Winter Haven, Florida. I hadn't seen my teammates since I got hurt, really. Not too many people from the team kept in touch except for the medical staff that kept sending me messages saying I had to do this and that.

To get to spring training, I got a ride to Detroit and flew to Tampa, which is only maybe an hour from Winter Haven. The team had a driver pick me up, and the entire time he asked about how I was doing. It was, "How are you feeling, Fergie?" and, "How you doing?" and, "How's your rehab coming?" Actually, I felt pretty good. I told him I couldn't skip, but I could run.

When I got to spring training, they told me I didn't have to go all out right away. The idea was for me to get stronger by just jogging to the outfield, not sprinting. The first couple of weeks in Florida were okay. The ankle would swell up, and I would ice it. It was all about working out without throwing. Don Zimmer didn't rush me, and neither did the ballclub. It was even mentioned that if I had to start the season on the disabled list, that was just part of the injury and recovery process.

For the first 20 days of spring training, I just ran and built my stamina, still nursing the Achilles tendon. Finally, I went to the bullpen mound to throw. My arm was fine, but it felt as if I was pushing it with the Achilles. That was the first time I put on spikes, too. I hadn't worn a regular baseball shoe since the preceding summer.

Wearing the spikes didn't feel good at all. I kept taking Tylenol and then I added in some Darvon. Darvon is a narcotic. I took Darvon and I didn't feel so bad. I began taking Darvon whenever I was supposed to throw, and I was throwing okay. I started pitching in exhibition games, and I got people out. Two weeks before the end of spring training, I was selected as the Opening Day pitcher. I was getting people out, and things were going smoothly. I really was surprised. Of course, the Red Sox didn't really know that my ankle was swelling up every time I worked out, that I had to use ice, and I was eating Darvon to control the pain. I put ice on my ankle at the end of the day and overnight, and in the morning the swelling would be down. I worked out again, and it swelled up again.

I was not like a young colt—the young colt was back home—but things were looking better. I kept telling myself, "Hey, with the work I did, I am proving people wrong. I am doing the right thing to get ready for the season."

Opening Day of 1977 we played the Indians. I came out of the game after allowing one earned run in 7⅔ innings, and we were ahead. But the bullpen lost the lead, and we lost the game. I got a no-decision. The fans were glad to see me. I got a standing ovation.

After the game, my dad wrote me a nice letter. I got cards and notes from fans who wished me good luck. My leg stopped bothering me. The ankle stopped swelling up. But I still iced it for six months. I was pitching pretty well, but it took me a few starts to get a win. And then it seemed as if Don Zimmer lost confidence in me.

He lost confidence in all of the guys in the Buffalo Head Gang, and at the end of the season, when I finished 10–10, I became a free agent. The Red Sox didn't want me anymore. But I felt I had more in me. I had worked so hard to come back, and I proved that I could still throw after the Achilles injury. I felt I could do better if someone gave me a chance. I had been determined that the Achilles injury would not end my career, and it didn't. Now I wanted to show I could win like the old Fergie.

It was a good thing I didn't burn any bridges when I left Texas, because the Rangers wanted me back. They offered me a new home for the 1978 season when they traded pitcher John Poloni and cash for me on December 14, 1977.

19

Back in Texas

After the 1977 season, the Red Sox essentially said, "You're not going to pitch anymore." But they were wrong. Texas had different plans for me. The manager then was Billy Hunter. He asked me, "Do you think you can help us in the bullpen?"

Of course I preferred to be a starter, but at that point I wanted to be on a major-league roster. Then Doc Medich came down with a sore arm, and I got moved into the rotation. I hardly pitched the first month of the season, but I finished 18-8. If I had had a few more starts, I could have won 20 games again. They weren't really sure how much I could still pitch. I was back from the Achilles injury.

Brad Corbett was the owner of the Rangers, and he signed me to a longer contract once I showed I could still be a winning pitcher. Everything seemed to fall into place. Most people identify me as a player with the Cubs, but in two stays I spent six years with the Texas Rangers. I won 93 games for them, and I am in the Rangers Hall of Fame.

Moving back into a team's starting rotation and winning those 18 games was very satisfying for me. It wasn't a vendetta against the Red Sox or other teams that didn't think I could still pitch, but I proved things to myself.

If anything, I did more fishing with Texas my second time around than I did anywhere else in my career. There were a series of five lakes around the Dallas area. I bought a boat and went fishing on the day I was scheduled to start. It didn't tire me out, it relaxed me. Jim Kern and Sparky Lyle went along a lot of the time. I picked the lake the night before, and there was a Country Kitchen restaurant centrally located. I announced to the players that anyone who wanted to fish with me the next morning should meet me for breakfast at 4:15 AM.

I went to bed right after the night game and set my alarm for 4:00 AM. I just rolled out of bed, pulled on shorts, a T-shirt, and running shoes, and I was ready to go. I had the boat loaded up in the parking lot. Whoever showed up at the Country Kitchen went with me. We got off the lake at 2:00 PM and made it to the ballpark in plenty of time.

We had some great guys on the team and some great players, even though we didn't win very much. Dock Ellis was there, and he was a colorful guy. He was a pretty good pitcher, and a flashy dresser. He did the earring thing, and not too many people had seen it at the time. It was relaxed, low-key fishing.

I also fished on the road. One time on a road trip to Minneapolis, four of us were going fishing. Unlike my announce-it-in-the-locker-room trips, this was prearranged with a guide supplying all of the rods and reels. Meet in the hotel lobby at 5:00 AM and head out. Dock Ellis got wind of the trip and decided he really, really wanted to go. Dock went shopping and bought all kinds of gear, a heavy jacket, boots, and came down to the hotel lobby at 3:30 AM to wait for us. There was only room for two fishermen in each boat, but we got it worked out.

It was April, so it was before the official bass fishing season opener. We couldn't keep any of the fish. It was catch-and-release. We were catching bass one after the other, but Dock didn't want to throw the fish back in the water. We kept telling him it was illegal to keep the fish, and he had to throw them back. He kept insisting, "No. I'm keeping them and taking them back to the hotel and cooking them up." By then, he had three or four fish on a stringer. We kept telling him, "Dock, you've got to release these fish. It's not the season." He wouldn't listen. Dock got up to four fish on the stringer. The guide was playing it cool for the moment since the fish were still alive.

We had a game that night, but none of us fishing were scheduled to pitch. It got to be about 3:30 PM, and we had to go in. We pleaded with Dock: "You've got to put these fish back. You can't take them with you. When we get back to the dock, there's going to be a game warden. They're going to lock up the whole boat because you've got fish in the boat."

The guide said, "Hey, Dock, you want some fish? I've got some fish in the freezer. I'll give you some of those to take back with you." Dock said, "No. I want these. I caught these. I caught these fish, and I ain't throwing them back." We were almost back to the dock and gave it another try: "Dock, please. You're going to get us all in trouble. You've got to turn these fish loose." Dock started swearing up and down, but he finally threw the fish in the water.

He stomped back to the truck and said, "I'm never fishing with you guys again." He was mad at everybody. On the ride from the lake to the hotel, Dock wouldn't speak to anybody. Later, the outfitter brought Dock a bunch of fillets. He felt a little bit better, but boy, was he mad that he had to throw back those bass.

My second time in Texas I became very good friends with Gaylord Perry. Gaylord, who played 22 years in the majors, and won 314 games, came and went from Texas twice, too. We were the graybeards of the squad, two pitchers who had been around a long time who thought we could still contribute. He was just a fun guy to be with. He was a bit crusty, but he had seen it all in his career. We talked a lot of baseball and enjoyed each other's company. And we ended up going into the Hall of Fame together, something we hoped would happen.

My second year in Texas my second time around, I had a record of 16–14. The next year I finished 12–12. The third season, 1981, was supposed to be our year. We were playing good baseball. But that was the year we ended up playing a split season and missing all those games in the middle of the year because of a labor battle with the owners. The Rangers had the second-best record in the West to Oakland in the first half and finished third in the second half.

The majority of the guys stayed around Arlington during the labor action. We worked out every day, took batting practice, and threw. We were hoping the disruption would be over within 10 days, but it dragged on and on. Finally, guys wanted to go home. When it got up to 50 days, I was on the other side of the mountain, too. Season's over, I'm going back to Canada.

Most of the disagreement was over benefits, and I wasn't sure that they were the correct issues to take a stand over at that time. The union wanted us to stick together. That spoiled the season for the Rangers. The labor problems ruined the season, and I finished 5-8.

That team had some good players. Sunny (Jim Sundberg) was still catching. Buddy Bell was there, Sparky Lyle. But things started to fall apart after the labor difficulties. We went through a few managers in a hurry. One of them managed one day—one day!

At that point in my career, I had 264 wins. When I was younger, I never thought so far ahead as to have a goal of winning 300 games. When I got 250 wins—I was with the Rangers—I started to think that maybe I had chance to do it. When I reached 270 wins, I looked at it that I need two more good years, winning 15 games in each year.

But I was not going to win those games in Texas. They were house-cleaning, looking to build with a young team. I knew I could still pitch, but it was a question of who wanted me.

I was turning 39 in the off-season after the end of the messed-up 1981 season, and I was a free agent. I was in the job market. I didn't have any links to any major-league team, but I did truly believe I could still pitch and that I could still help someone. I was not ready to retire, but I had not even spoken to my agent yet as the World Series ended.

One day in the middle of November, I got a phone call from Dallas Green, whom of course I had known in Philadelphia, but by then was running the Cubs. He said, "Ferguson, do you still want to pitch?"

I said, "Of course."

Dallas said the team was young and had a lot of young pitchers, but no veterans, and he wanted some experience on the staff. "We'd like to sign you to a contract." I signed a one-year contract, and that's how I ended up back with the Cubs in 1982. I thought if I could finish my career with the Cubs, and pitch in Wrigley Field again in front of those great Chicago fans, it would be icing on the cake. I was certain of one thing. The calendar might say that I was aging, but my arm was still young. I once told a reporter that as soon as I pulled on a baseball uniform, my arm was convinced it was 25.

My time spent in Texas was something I enjoyed very much, but an experience that muddied my reputation while I was pitching for the Rangers was extremely disturbing. It carried a lifetime taint, and even now, nearly 30 years after the incident, people don't understand what happened.

20

End of Playing Days

In November of 1980, I was arrested in Toronto. When my suitcase was searched after a trip, I was charged with possession of small amounts of marijuana, hashish, and cocaine. I was stunned by the situation. I did not put drugs in my suitcase and did not know what was going on.

Things got very strange. I have contended that I was set up for this arrest and that I committed no crimes. I am pretty sure that I know who did it, but that is not something I will reveal publicly. I ended up being charged, tried, and convicted, but the judge set aside my sentence and erased the conviction.

A lot of people who only heard parts of the case got it in their heads that I was a drug addict or a criminal. And even though the record was cleared, unfortunately, some people think of me as a lawbreaker caught up in the drug culture. Those who followed the case realized I was not a criminal, but even now, decades later, some people just immediately react when they hear my name and blame me for being involved with drugs.

I was arrested on August 25, during the baseball season, on a road trip that was taking us from Milwaukee into Canada. The Rangers took a chartered plane, but luggage belonging to four people connected to the team, myself, Mickey Rivers, Frank Lucchesi, and a clubhouse boy who was on his first road trip, was not placed on the plane. The luggage was missing from Toronto International Airport for more than a day. It didn't arrive later that night or the next day. Eventually, the suitcases turned up. Under Canadian law, the bags had to be opened by the customs service because the owners of the luggage were not present.

The customs people called us at the hotel and asked for permission to open the bags. I felt I had nothing to hide and gave permission. Then I went to the ballpark for a Rangers game. However, at the park I was arrested and charged. I was dismayed by the whole situation. The arrest itself, in front of the team, was humiliating. The agents even watched me take a shower.

I was taken back to the hotel and asked the whereabouts of my hang-up suit bag. That perplexed me because I didn't own one or use one. My suitcase was locked, but my valuables pouch from the ballpark was in it. It contained my wallet and credit cards, but they should have been locked up at the park, not in my suitcase. I had no idea how that stuff got there. Only one person had the keys to the valuables room when we were playing. I didn't really want to do interviews after I got arrested, but I did talk to one reporter from my home town. I wanted the people of Chatham to hear me out and be on my side even though I was embarrassed by the entire episode. Even when I talked to the reporter from my home town, I said I couldn't tell the whole story. I didn't know how the stuff got into my suitcase, but I didn't blame it on anyone else.

Not long after that, I was summoned to meet with Baseball Commissioner Bowie Kuhn. This was very awkward because the case was still pending, and under Canadian law, whatever was said in a proceeding with Kuhn could be used against me in court. The commissioner was told this, but he insisted on meeting with me, anyway. Among the questions they wanted to ask me were: whom I supplied with drugs, what other players used drugs, and where I got the drugs. Despite being informed I could not answer his questions at the time, Kuhn suspended me for not answering the questions.

The Rangers filed a grievance on my behalf. The team was fighting for second place and wanted me to play. An official baseball arbitrator ruled that Kuhn was wrong, that he should not have suspended me, and that my suspension should immediately be lifted. Red Smith, the famous sports columnist for The New York Times, wrote that Kuhn had prejudged me and essentially convicted me of the drug charges even though the Canadian court had not. He said that Kuhn was arbitrarily using his power.

When the case came to court in Brampton, Ontario, I was con-victed of being in possession of four grams of cocaine. The charges of being in possession of marijuana and hashish were dropped. The truth was, I had used drugs recreationally, not heavily, not a lot, but as a fun thing like alcohol at parties. I was definitely not an addict or a drug dealer. It was a mistake. Sometimes you do things in your life that you know are wrong, but you do them anyway. The moral of that is to not do wrong things at all, and not have to regret it later.

I had plenty of time to think after I got arrested and charged, while waiting for the court case to start, and waiting for its resolution. It felt as if I had been to hell and back by the time it was resolved. I did feel good that there were so many witnesses willing to speak up on my behalf.

The judge heard testimony from a large number of character wit-nesses who said they couldn't imagine me selling drugs and that I had always been an exemplary member of the community who helped out worthy causes. The conviction could have carried a maximum penalty of six months in jail and $1,000 fine. However, just an hour into his deliberations, Judge Jerry Young put aside the conviction and erased it from my record. The legal term was "an absolute discharge." The effect of that action was as if I had not been convicted. It was clear to me that the judge heard the case and suspected there was more to the story than just me being a bad guy. I was really innocent and set up. At the time, I was scared that my entire life would be ruined and my reputation would be smeared.

If the conviction had stood with the penalty, that would have ended my major-league baseball career. I would not have been able to travel back and forth to play ball. I am sure Bowie Kuhn would have reinstated his suspension, too. At the time, I had 259 victories, and that's how things would have ended. As it was, I missed two weeks of play in September while the suspension was in effect.

Bowie Kuhn was not done, either. After the court case was over, and leading up to spring training, he required me to donate $10,000 to a drug education and prevention program in Texas specifically targeting young people. He said I would have to appear in an anti-drug baseball film and participate in a Major League Baseball anti-drug education program. And I had to cooperate with a Texas Rangers' anti-drug education program. I was fine with all of that, and I agreed.

Something like that sticks to you, though. People think if they read it in the newspaper it must be true, and they remember, "Oh, Fergie Jenkins, didn't he have a drug problem of some type?" I was cleared, but people don't really remember. Unfortunately, those items were found in my suitcase.

For a long time, not even my dad believed that they weren't mine. I kept telling him, "Dad, I am a winning pitcher in the big leagues. How can I win by taking all of these drugs? There's no way I'm taking drugs." It took a while for him to start believing me. That hurt, especially when it's your own flesh and blood doubting you.

The drug incident took place in 1980, and I continued to pitch with the Rangers through the 1981 season. When I became a free agent again, I do not know if some teams ignored me because of the drug case. It could not have helped, although I was cleared. The Cubs were the number-one team for me to go back to, anyway. I do believe that the drug case hurt my election to the Hall of Fame. It may have delayed my receiving the 75 percent of the votes cast. I'm sure some of the voters held it against me. I'm sure they didn't know the whole story about the verdict being erased. I worried that I might never be elected and that the drug case would be the reason. I was on the ballot a couple of times before I was selected. There was enough of a delay that I was concerned. But I never got into any trouble again with drugs or anything else, so my record was clean when the voters selected me.

Even now, once in a while, somebody brings it up. They say, "Didn't you get busted?" And I say, "Yeah, they found some articles in my suitcase in 1980." Thirty years later, and I still hear about it. It doesn't annoy me as much as you might think. I was in the wrong place at the wrong time, and unfortunately those things were in my suitcase, and I have to live with it.

My problem did not prevent me from hooking up with the Cubs again, however. I still had the desire to pitch and wanted to win 300 games. Courtesy of Dallas Green, I rejoined the Cubs for the 1982 season. This was a new-look Cubs. The mainstays of the team when I was winning 20 games were gone. They were looking forward to a new generation of players moving in.

I worked hard in spring training, and I was the starting pitcher for the Cubs' home opener. Who would have ever thought I'd be in that role for the Cubs again? The Cubs were not very good that year. We finished 73–89. My pitching record was 14–15. I had some no-decisions. I had only signed a one-year contract, but after the season, the Cubs invited me to come back. We both seemed to think it would be pretty cool for me to win my 300th game with the Cubs.

Only in 1983 I pitched a lot less, and some of that was coming out of the bullpen. Lee Elia was the manager, and that was the season he went on that rant that everyone still remembers. He just let loose and blasted the fans one day after they were booing some of the players. I finished 6–9. It was an up-and-down year.

One of the neat things that I accomplished my second time around with the Cubs was breaking the 3,000-strikeout barrier. For decades, the record had been held by Walter Johnson, and only a few pitchers passed 3,000. Now Nolan Ryan has the record with 5,714 strikeouts, but 3,000 is still the key number, like getting 3,000 hits if you are a batter.

I finished my career with 3,192 strikeouts and passed 3,000 in 1982, the year before I retired. I am 12th on the all-time list, and only 16 guys have ever struck out 3,000 hitters. It's a nice distinction.

A lot of the pitchers who struck out 3,000 batters were considered power pitchers. I was not. It's about control. The pitchers who came along after Walter Johnson, who had 3,509 strikeouts and retired in 1927, had more variety of pitches at their command. They used sliders and sinkers, as well as curves and fastballs. They had four or more pitches to fool batters. A lot of us also pitched a lot of years.

The Cubs had a bunch of young players—Lee Smith, Ryne Sandberg, Jody Davis. They were the building blocks. I was coming back for the 1984 season—which was a fun one in Chicago since the Cubs won a division title—with the idea of trying to win 300 games. Then in spring training I pitched about two innings. In mid-March I was released. They said maybe I could negotiate a deal with another team before the regular season started. I said, "I don't want to pitch for anybody else."

That was me being hurt and angry. I wanted to finish my career as a Cub. I could have gone to Pittsburgh or Los Angeles, but I got a plane ticket home and never looked back. That was it. I could have still played. I could have worked out for somebody else, but I wanted to finish my career as a Cub. So I did. I regretted it later. I had 284 wins, and I needed 16 more. I could have hit 300 with another club. I could still pitch. There was nothing wrong with my arm. I got home March 10 and was fishing March 11. I fished for a couple of days. I had never been home for the pickerel run.

The Indians phoned me twice, trying to get me to join Cleveland. I said no. I do wonder what would have happened if I had pitched a little bit longer. Gaylord Perry stuck around to get his 300th win. I probably should have done it. That was the year I was urged to run for political office at home, and I did that and concentrated on my farm. I lost the election, so that was the end of my political career. It was also the end of my major-league baseball career.

21

Hunting and Fishing

I have been involved in fishing and hunting longer than I have been involved in baseball. My dad took me fishing to Lake Erie for the first time when I was about five.

That time, I mostly sat and watched on a pier, but I was too antsy to sit still. I got up and was looking around. There was some moss on the cement, and I slipped. I fell into the water, but my dad grabbed me by the back of the neck and pulled me up. My mother called me "Little Fergie," but I can tell you that's not what my dad called me at the time.

We sometimes fished off a tugboat in Lake Erie. They had tugboats docked in a small canal. We could walk along the inland harbor and fish. We brought worms or minnows and fished from our spots and caught perch and bluegill. It was nice quality time with my dad, shared time together. My dad and I spent a lot of time together. I was an only child, and my mom and my dad both spent a lot of time with me.

My mom fished, too. She had her own fishing rod. My dad caught fish and loved eating them. He liked preparing fish, too, and he had some very tasty fish dishes.

I was about 12 when I first went hunting. My dad and a friend of his, Kenny Price, went on a rabbit hunt, and I was sort of the bird dog. Along with the real dogs, that is. Kenny Price had two little beagles. We were hunting in a lot of brush piles. The dogs were sniffing underneath, and I was stomping on the top. The rabbits ran out, and *boom! boom!* Kenny and my dad shot a couple of rabbits. After they shot them, they stuffed them into a backpack that I wore.

That was my introduction to hunting. A year or so later, I got to handle a gun. It was a 12-gauge shotgun. I really felt like a hunter because I had my own gun. The first animal I hunted was rabbit, too, then pheasants. And I progressed to ducks. Ducks were a challenge. I think it helped my hand-eye coordination to be able to hit a rabbit that was running in the brush. It was a tough shot to try when it was running down a ditch bank.

I had a paper route, and when I saved a little bit of money, I bought a better shotgun. When I signed my contract with the Phillies, I bought myself some more guns, name brands like Remington and Winchester. When I really started to make some money I invested in Weatherbys. I bought a .300 Weatherby Magnum, and I went moose hunting. I bought a .270. These were guns with more power, which I knew were capable of bringing down the kind of game that I wanted to shoot. I bought the .270 for deer, a 7 millimeter for elk. It was a matter of knowing the guns and reading up on them and understanding the caliber I needed for hunting the particular animal. Hunting became a lifelong hobby.

I tried to get my boy Raymond involved in hunting. He likes to fish. He didn't like to hunt. A couple of times we sat in a deer stand, and he got cold. He didn't like to sit and be patient. I got Raymond the right type of cold-weather boots, but he's the type of individual who doesn't like to sit still. It was the same thing in a boat at first, but he overcame that, and we caught a lot of fish together. He liked fishing at the ponds in Canada and on lakes.

When I was playing with the Cubs, Billy Williams and I liked to fish together. We owned a 25-foot Chris-Craft together. We bought it from a retired police officer. In our era, we played all those day games, so we had some time to go out fishing. We had a couple of hours after a game. The boat was docked at Burnham Harbor in Chicago, and we got out on Lake Michigan.

We'd get out of the locker room and only take the boat out a few miles. Lake Michigan is a big lake, and we didn't want to get caught in a storm. We got caught up in some of those big waves, but never a bad storm. We picked a spot a couple of miles offshore and tried to corral a school of fish. Then we trolled for them. Billy was a hunter, too, and in the off-season I joined him in Alabama deer hunting. We also went to Newfoundland together to hunt moose one November.

The trip began by flying into really remote areas. We had a helicopter pilot take us to a distant cabin. On the way we saw a lot of moose not too far away. That night, however, it snowed 17 inches. We had a film crew with us for an outdoors show, and we set out the next morning trying to find one of those moose. We saw one, but there was no clear shot, so I didn't take it. The last thing you want to do is wound a moose in thick cover. If you wound him, you've got to trail him for miles and miles. If you're trailing them for miles, you might not find them until the next day.

Back at the cabin, we enjoyed a rum alcohol drink that we diluted a little with Pepsi-Cola. We were getting pretty happy. It snowed even more. The snow was so high we couldn't get out the front door. Our outfitter climbed out the window and shoveled the door clear so we could get out of the cabin. We were up there for four or five days, but we didn't have any hunting success.

I have shot moose on other trips in Ontario. There's an area where I've shot some moose and a lot of deer. I ate the moose meat. It's good, but it's a little tough. Like antelope meat. Antelope meat is a little less gamy. But if you shoot a deer and soak it in vinegar overnight, it removes the gamy taste. Then put the tenderloin part in thin slabs and make stew with fried rice. Deer is really tender if you prepare it the right way, and so are elk, antelope, and moose. I haven't shot a bear. I would like to. I've seen plenty of them.

Once, I went black bear hunting in Pennsylvania, but the bear was just a little bit too far off for me to get a good shot. So I didn't really have a chance. I have hunted in a lot of places where there were bears and we saw them, but bears weren't the game I was hunting.

Jody Davis, the former Cubs catcher who is managing in their minor league system, and I have hunted a lot together. We've hunted together in Canada, South Dakota, Iowa, and near Roanoke, Virginia, mostly for whitetail deer. I have hunted with Bill Buckner in Idaho, where he lives. Billy's a good shot and he loves to fish. Lee Smith loves to fish, too.

Illinois is a great place to hunt deer. It's been growing in popularity. It seems like there are a million deer in Oklahoma. Texas has a lot of deer. There are more deer everywhere. There's been an explosion in the population. I've hunted in a lot of different states. I try to diversify. If you have been in an area before you hunt, it helps. Or if you have an outfitter who knows the terrain and gives you a topographical map, you can work with that.

When you are deer hunting in different places, you get different weather. If you are hunting in October, you don't get snow. If you hunt in late November or December, you can run into snow. The farther west you go—to North Dakota, Idaho, and Wyoming—the earlier you get snow.

I don't mind hunting in snow or in heavy frost. If you have the proper clothing, Gore-Tex, and weatherproof items, the right kind of gloves, and you keep your feet warm, you should be okay. I do all of the meticulous things to get ready for hunting. Scent-free clothing, carbon free. I own a scent-free bag where I put dirt in and leave it with the clothes for a week at a time before the hunt and then again each night. Although I do a lot of bow hunting, I have some good guns. Bellini makes good guns, Remington. I know that some shotguns, with gold inlay, can sell for $100,000. I don't have one of those. And I know you can get a cheap gun for $225. I want a good gun, but I don't want to spend thousands and thousands and thousands.

I have never been big-game hunting in Africa. I've talked about it but never went. I've never hunted polar bear and never hunted grizzly bear. Polar bears are dangerous. They're carnivorous, more so than a grizzly.

The late Red Fisher, the famous Canadian fishing guide, was a good friend. Once we were on a trip to Great Slave Lake in the Northwest Territories. We had a trout-catching contest going in the boat, and I was down one fish to Red. I was in the front of the boat. He was in the back of the boat. There were cameramen along in another boat. We went around a bend in the shore and saw all these birds circling overhead. There was a grizzly there.

We were far enough away, but we kept watch. Seagulls were dive-bombing for fish, and the bear was fishing, too. All of a sudden, I had a bite. The fish was on, maybe 100 yards up the shoreline. I got the fish hooked well, and it came up splashing. The bear looked up and started into the water.

At that point we were about 30 yards offshore, and I was reeling in the fish. The bear started swimming to the fish. The cameraman zoomed in on the grizzly. I was trying to get the fish into the boat so I could score more points than Red. There was a Cree Indian guide in the boat with us, and he was steering. The grizzly was within 10 feet of the boat when the guide put the boat into reverse really slowly.

The fish was right there. I almost had it. Suddenly, the bear stopped swimming. His head and shoulders were above the water, but he was in deep water. His feet weren't on the bottom, so he couldn't lunge for the fish. We backed up and I got the fish close to the boat and then I brought it in. Red said, "You win." The grizzly swam back to shore and ran up the shoreline. But just before it ran over a hill, it turned around and looked back at us. That long and thin trout weighed about seven or eight pounds. To tell you the truth, when the bear went back to shore, I thought he was more nervous than we were.

The biggest fish I ever caught was a 55-pound king salmon. I was fishing in Alaska, on the Kenai River, where the world record of 97¼ pounds was caught. I was there with John Havlicek, the former Boston Celtics star, his son Chris, and Tom Seaver. It was all catch-and-release. We caught a couple of 35-pounders one day, and John caught a 60-pounder. The next day I caught the 55-pounder, but it wasn't even the biggest fish on the trip.

Canada is a tremendous place to fish. I have fished in a lot of places in the country, from the Northwest Territories to the Yukon Territory. There's a place in the Yukon with a lot of grayling that have dorsal fins, so they look like flying fish. They run maybe four pounds. They make an excellent shore lunch. It's a nice challenge to catch them on fly rods with little dry flies.

I have looked into a polar bear hunt, but it won't be before 2010. Jody Davis wants to hunt Kodiak brown bear in Alaska with a bow, and I would be his backup. It's at least a $5,000 trip, depending on how long you go for, plus the travel, the lodge, and the license. It could be $8,000, or if you add a moose tag, it might be $10,000.

To hunt polar bears, you have to go way north, probably to Nunavut. You've got to go out on the ice floes with a guide on a snowmobile or a dog sled. I've got all of the right clothing. It's a day hunt, and you have to camp and spend time in a tent. You hunt on the move each day, trying to trail them. Even if I got one, I probably wouldn't be able to have the mount in the house. My wife doesn't want dead animal heads around. When I had my farmhouse, I had about 30 taxidermy mounts and trophies. I had whitetail deer, elk, mule deer, turkey, a big goose, a lot of fish—I had a 14-pound bass—a coyote, a bobcat, a boar, and a goat. I gave them all away. People dream of catching a 20-pound bass. I hear the best place to go for them now is Mexico. There are places in Mexico where you can catch 100 large-mouth bass a day.

I shot a goat in Texas, a certain kind that was imported from India. It was black, a beautiful animal, a wooly goat. In the goat's habitat, the natives catch them, take off their hair, and weave it into blankets and coats.

The goat was on private land, a 20,000-acre place that had a lot of African animals on it. I shot the goat at about 280 yards with my .270 rifle. I hit it right in the shoulder. He went right down, and that was it. I'm lucky that it didn't roll another 15 feet because he was on top of a cliff, and I would have had to climb down another 200 feet to get him. I mounted it from the shoulders up.

Bill Buckner—this was after he retired from the Cubs and the Red Sox—and I were on a hunt in the mountains in Idaho. We drove to 8,500 feet and then we rode horses higher along these switchbacks. The horses were all lathered up, but we saw elk at about 11,000 feet. Walking at that altitude was pretty tough at first, but we got used to it. It got to be around 6:30 in the evening, and we had our bows out. Bill had shot a small bull earlier in the week, skinned it, and put it in the freezer of a truck that was kept at the campsite.

It was November, and it had been unseasonably warm. Bill had a good sleeping bag and so did I. In his wisdom, Billy said, "We'll just zipper up and sleep under the stars." I said, "Buck, we need to put up the tent." He replied, "Oh, no, we'll sleep under the stars." It had not snowed at that elevation yet that year. The moon came out at about 7:30. It took us 30 minutes to put up the tent. We picked our spots in the tent, sleeping opposite ways in the two-man tent, but at 4:30 AM I had to get up to go to the bathroom. I opened up the flap, and everything was covered in white. Welcome to winter.

I went out in my stocking feet, prancing all around. When I got back to the tent, I woke Billy. I said, "Buck, good thing we put up the tent." We got up for the day at 6:00 AM, and it was cold. The sun came out, but it was really cold. We looked around for game that morning, didn't find anything, and retreated from the mountains. Buck gives me credit for that one. "You used your head," he said. I was thinking about the Boy Scout motto of being prepared.

When we got lower, I saw an elk, but it was about 800 yards away, too far. There was a lot of snow lower down, and I wondered about the horses' footing on those switchbacks. We had to put our trust in them. At one point along a cliff wall, the drop was right there, about 200 feet. My horse was sure-footed. At another point, the last horse wanted to pass. That was crazy. I dismounted and said, "Hey, Buck, put this horse in the middle." The horse just didn't want to be trailing. We had a five-day adventure, but we lived to tell about it.

A little more than a year ago, I shot a huge deer, an eight-pointer. I was hunting with Len Barker, the former Indians pitcher who threw a perfect game, and we were right near the Cleveland airport. We were bow hunting, separated a bit from each other in tree stands. I took the shot from about 25 yards. I first saw the big buck behind some tree limbs. Then he put his head around a tree briefly and edged his whole body out in front of a bush. I got the shot, and it went right through him. It was a good shot. The arrow went right through his neck.

I climbed down from the tree stand and waited for the deer to move. I got closer and closer, but he wasn't moving ever again. I walked up on him and flipped one leg over. The buck was dead on the spot.

Lenny's tree was close enough for me to see by glassing it with binoculars. I gutted out the deer. I thought I would lighten him by taking out his internal parts and then maybe I could turn him over and drag him back to the tree stand. But I couldn't drag that monster 10 feet through the leaves.

I waited another hour to see if Lenny got anything. I didn't hear anything, but when I glassed, I could see he was out of the tree stand. So I thought it was safe to shout without scaring off any deer he spotted. I yelled, "Hey, Lenny!" I heard back, "Yeah, what?" I said, "I've got one down." He shouted, "Big one?" I said, "Medium." I figured I would surprise him.

It took Lenny about 20 minutes to circle around in the bush and catch up to me. I saw him coming, and he asked, "Where's he at?" I said the deer was downed in the brush. When he walked up to the deer and looked down, he went, "God damn, that ain't a medium!"

We went to retrieve the ATV, and it took both us to load that deer meat on the back. It was a task holding the deer steady. That deer weighed 262 pounds dressed.

22

Oh, Canada

I was the first Canadian to be inducted into the Baseball Hall of Fame, but I was not the first Canadian to play in the majors by any means. There were players who preceded me, players who were contemporaries, and players who succeeded me.

According to the Canadian Baseball Hall of Fame, where I am a member, the first documented Canadian to play major-league baseball was a guy named Mike Brannock from Guelph in 1871. Ironically, he played for Chicago between 1871 and 1875. Arthur Irwin, 1880, and his brother John, 1882, from Toronto, were two of the earliest Canadian major leaguers.

It is said that if he didn't exactly invent the baseball glove that Arthur Irwin did a great deal to popularize the idea of using a glove instead of bare hands to catch a ball. He came up with the idea because he broke two fingers and wanted additional padding on his hand to protect the injured area.

Canada is a large country in area, but it is a small place in population. There are about the same number of Canadians as there are Californians. So if someone is making his mark in baseball, I am going to be aware of it.

Pitcher Claude Raymond was around in the majors when I was playing and so was Johnny Upham, Reno Bertoia, and Reggie Cleveland. There was not a big crowd of us, but there were Canadians playing at the top level of the game. We were all proud to represent our country. I still am the first and only Canadian in the Baseball Hall of Fame, and I was the first Cy Young Award winner. More recently, Eric Gagne won the Cy Young Award after his great season pitching in relief. He is French-Canadian. In-between, Larry Walker won the batting title, and he was on the All-Star team about a half dozen times.

Sometimes I wonder if American baseball fans who didn't follow my career closely realize I am not an American citizen. It doesn't come up much, but I reinforce the fact that I am still Canadian. That's my heritage. Believe me, in Canada, everyone knows I'm Canadian. I make a lot of appearances in Canada with other Canadian athletes. We get to know one another regardless of what sport we played. There just aren't as many Canadian sports heroes as there are Americans. There are fewer Olympic medal winners. The population is so much smaller, maybe 10 percent of the United States.

In 1968 there was a huge gathering of athletes who were invited to participate in the dedication of the newly renovated Montreal Forum where the Canadiens play their National Hockey League games. I was there. Maurice "Rocket" Richard, John Ferguson, many of the old Canadiens players, and the figure skater Barbara Ann Scott were all part of it. I dropped the puck at Maple Leaf Gardens, too, when they opened the new building. I got to meet a lot of the old stars like Dave Keon, George Armstrong, and Red Kelly. I thought it was interesting that they invited someone that was better known for another sport, but I was Canadian, from Ontario, and fairly popular. People knew my name.

Over the years, I met a lot of the big Canadian hockey stars. Many times we were at banquets or charity fundraisers together. It was always fun for me because I had been a hockey fan growing up and remembered when they played. I met Gordie Howe (Mr. Hockey), Rocket Richard, Bobby Orr, and Johnny Bucyk. For a while, it seemed as if I knew more hockey players than baseball players. Doug Harvey was always my number-one hero whom I cheered for as a kid. He played that hard-nosed defense, and then Bobby Orr changed the game, put the offense into the defense, with his speed and puck-handling.

That's how I played hockey. I was a rushing defenseman like Orr, only without his great ability. He was one of the five best hockey players of all time. I skated well, shot the puck hard, played aggressively, and

172

made all the right moves. But as I look back, I am not sure I could have been successful as a hockey player. I certainly would not have reached the level I did in baseball. My baseball friends won't like this comment, but I still look on hockey as a greater challenge than baseball. You have to learn more techniques in hockey, such as stick-handling, maneuvering on the ice on two thin blades, and playing defense. Or maybe my perspective is skewed because I was better in baseball. It is often said that the most difficult thing to do in sports is to hit a baseball. I was basically on the other side of the equation, the guy throwing the ball.

When I played for the Cubs in Chicago, I sometimes worked out with the Blackhawks. They had Bobby and Dennis Hull at the time. Dale Tallon, who is now general manager of the Blackhawks, used to lend me his stick. I saw him quite a bit. I still see him at golf outings. I'm glad to see the Blackhawks on the rise again. They're making a comeback with all the kids they have.

When I was playing in the majors, I tried to return to Chatham for part of the off-season. I always visited my parents when they were still alive. I participated in charity events when invited and still make a lot of appearances all over Canada. I do not have dual U.S.-Canadian citizenship. I live in the United States, but I have what is called a permanent resident visa.

There was more than one occasion when people in Chatham and the people of Canada reminded me of how proud they were of what I had accomplished in baseball. I was honored several times with special awards. During the winter of 1972, after I won 24 games and was presented the Cy Young Award as the best pitcher in the National League, the city of London, Ontario, celebrated a Ferguson Jenkins Day. The mayor presented me with a scroll commemorating the day, and there was a huge banquet tied into fundraising for the London and District Crippled Children's Treatment Centre.

That same winter, the Chatham Kiwanis Club hosted a special Fergie event, too. One of my old coaches, Doug Allin, was the mayor, and he told a story about how one time I was ordered to do some extra running as punishment for not going hard in a hot day's workout. The coaches forgot about me, but I kept running and running.

A big thrill for me came a little bit later, in 1979, when I was presented with the Order of Canada. The public sends nominations to the governor-general, and the awards are given each year to Canadians for "distinguished service" in a field or area. Man, the Order of Canada. That was pretty special recognition.

There was a period of time that I actually got into politics. I had superb name recognition and the work seemed like a good challenge, so I ran for office in a provincial election for the Liberal Party. I lost. That was a short political career.

Hockey, as always, was the number-one sport in Canada, when I was playing baseball in the United States, and the biggest sports heroes in the country were hockey players. So I was very flattered and surprised in 1967 when I was chosen Canada's outstanding male athlete. My closest competition in the vote was Bobby Hull, and I had a lot more difficulty registering the results of that election than I did the provincial one. "I beat Bobby?" is the first thing I said. Then I won again in 1968, 1971, and 1972.

In 1974 I won the Lou Marsh Memorial Trophy given annually to Canada's top athlete, amateur or professional, male or female. The award was initiated in 1936, and among the other winners were Terry Fox, who ran across Canada on one leg to raise money for cancer research, and Wayne Gretzky. My presentation took place at Jarry Park before a baseball game between Montreal and San Diego. What a great honor that was. In 1987 I was also inducted into the Canadian Sports Hall of Fame. And I was part of the pioneer class of athletes chosen for the Ontario Sports Legends Hall of Fame.

I am also pleased to say that there is a baseball field located in St. Mary's in Southwestern Ontario named after me.

Another very cool thing that happened to me was being selected for inclusion in Canada's Walk of Fame in Toronto. The whole operation resembles the Hollywood Walk of Fame in California, where celebrities put their hands or feet in cement with their signatures. Among some of the others in the Walk of Fame are Gordie Howe, Donald Sutherland, William Shatner, and Michael J. Fox. My guest presenter was Gene Dziadura.

At the ceremony, there was a video shown of my life, and I got very choked up at the pictures of my mom and dad. I was very emotional, and I could hardly stand. I also knocked the 30-pound trophy onto the floor. The trophy featured a large star, and the unfortunate bounce bent one point. I tried to recover by making a joke, saying, "Good thing I wasn't a shortstop."

American baseball fans may not realize how I have maintained my ties and connections to Chatham, Ontario, and Canada, but Canadians understand that I always considered myself Canadian first and never considered obtaining a U.S. passport.

In fact, I put down more roots in Canada right in the middle of my streak of 20-game winning seasons with the Cubs. In 1972 I bought my first ranch in Blenheim, Ontario, which is only about eight miles from Chatham. It was 100 acres. I had signed a good contract the year before that had a lot of incentive clauses. I got a $50,000 bonus if I did this, a $10,000 bonus if I did that. These included things like pitching 300 innings. Well, I made most of the bonus money, and I used it to make a down payment on a ranch, and the family moved to Blenheim. I kept the old silo and began putting more buildings on. I bulldozed an old, burned-out barn. Before I left for spring training in 1973, we had a nice, four-bedroom home with a circular driveway and land that was all fenced in.

When I was young, I had an uncle with a farm who raised pigs and chickens. I used to work for him on the weekends, and I liked it. Pigs and chickens are not very sweet-smelling animals, so I said to myself if I was going to farm or ever had a ranch I wanted to raise cattle or corn. And I thought a ranch was a great place to raise kids.

Kathy and I had three girls, and they helped me with the chores. They drove tractors. They entered 4-H competitions. Kimberly was really into farming. They enjoyed it all.

I started small, with 15 head of Angus cattle. I fed them to the point where they reached 800 or 900 pounds and then sold them and made a little bit of money. The next time, I bought 30 head of cattle. I did the same thing and sold them. I was basically fattening the cattle up for market. Then we had no animals on the ranch, so I bought two horses and enjoyed having them around. I decided to get my own dozen calves and a French bull. It was tan, kind of like the color of pancakes, and weighed around 1,800 pounds. The cows were a mix of Hereford and Angus—beef cows. I was instructed to breed the cows to the bull when they hit 600 or 700 pounds and this bull was good. He went 12-for-12, no problems. The bull had all the fun.

I really liked riding the horses. I installed a pasture in front of the house, about 10 acres worth, surrounded by a white-rail fence. I dug a four-acre pond in the back. I still had 40 acres of pasture, and I grew corn in back of the silo, trying to be a farmer, too. I wasn't much of a farmer the first couple of years, but I got better. I leased another 100 acres of land up the road and grew corn that I sold to Kellogg's. I got the cows up to 35 head, and everything went like clockwork.

A friend suggested artificial insemination. I was leery of getting into it, but eventually I bought a prize cow for $25,000 at an auction. I kept the old bull, too. I ended up using artificial insemination on nine of the cows, and they had calves within two or three days of one another. That actually made the local news.

The system was working so well, I bought another prize cow for $10,000 and got up to about 65 head of cattle. I started selling some decent animals, but that year people weren't buying a lot of cattle. I had trouble getting my veterinary fees back. There is a lot of work involved, and a lot of care taken, when you breed one purebred animal to another purebred animal.

After a while, it got to the point where I was doing a lot of work in the off-season, and I couldn't handle it all even with help. My father stayed there. I had a foreman in the field. I hired another kid whose father knew a lot about combines and machinery. I did a lot of work, but I made some money here and some money there. It was fun to do. I was making one of my childhood goals become reality, and I got a lot of satisfaction out of it. Farming and ranching occupied my time and my mind, and they certainly were different from baseball.

23

Personal Tragedies

My life has been blessed in so many ways, but I have also suffered through terrible tragedies that sometimes I wondered if I would survive. I did so only with the help and guidance of God.

Kathy and I had been together for two decades and had three lovely daughters when we split up. We had met in high school and got married in 1965. After I retired from baseball, we gradually grew apart. We separated in 1984 and were divorced in 1987, officially, after 23 years of marriage.

Around that time, I heard that Tony Lucadello, who had signed me to my first professional baseball contract, was diagnosed with cancer—pancreatic cancer or a tumor. I was never sure exactly what. But he didn't tell anyone, even his wife. Tony signed 52 guys who went on to play in the majors in a scouting career that began with the Cubs in 1943 and was transferred to the Phillies in 1957. Tony scouted for 46 years. He was 76 years old in 1989 when the Phillies told him they wouldn't need him the next season. On May 8, 1989, Tony drove over to the ballfields in Fostoria, Ohio, where he had scouted players over the years, and killed himself.

I got a call from Gene Dziadura, who said, "I've got some bad news." My mind raced at the time because I thought everyone I knew in Chatham was healthy. I don't know if it was that Tony didn't want to go through the suffering of cancer, or something else. Some people said he was heartbroken because the Phillies didn't want him anymore. So he killed himself. He was like a father to Gene, and it was a tremendous shock to a lot of people. There was a closed casket at the funeral.

Later on, the people in Fostoria named those baseball fields after Tony Lucadello, and they put up a monument to commemorate his contributions to baseball. The sign on the statue says, "Baseball's Friend."

There had been a lot of strain in my life, and after the divorce, I was disenchanted with women. I didn't even date for a while. I ended up meeting my second wife, Mary Anne, through a friend of mine named Ray Meyers. This was not the same guy who coached the DePaul college basketball team. My friend Ray invited me to attend a Chicago Bears game, and then we went out for a drink. It was a late-season game, and we were freezing. I was wearing a heavy coat and Sorel boots. The whole works.

Ray was a member of a darts team at a tavern on Lincoln Avenue. We went there and sat in a booth with Gary Miller, one of his teammates. Gary recognized me from the Cubs. We talked for a while, and then a women's darts team came in. One of the players was Mary Anne, Gary's sister. She asked if I would sign an autograph for her son. Raymond was four at the time. My friend Ray's team had a match, and about 20 minutes later Mary Anne came back over and said, "Why are you sitting all alone?" She said her team was just practicing, so why didn't I join them? I don't know how I did it because I didn't play darts, but I made a few bull's-eyes.

Mary Anne said, "You've got a pretty good knack for doing that." I said, "Maybe it's just luck." I hung out with them playing darts and had a few beers. She was a nice lady, and we exchanged phone numbers. We went out on some dates when I came back to see more Bears games. A little while after we got to know one another, Mary Anne brought Raymond and vacationed with me in Canada. I showed them around Ontario. In 1988 Mary Anne and I got married in Las Vegas. At first, Mary Anne moved to Canada with me, and we put Raymond in school there.

But the Rangers intervened. They asked if I wanted to be the pitching coach for one of their minor league teams in Oklahoma. That's how we ended up on a new, 160-acre ranch in Guthrie, Oklahoma. The ranch had been repossessed by the bank, so I got a good deal.

My first assignment was to repair the living quarters. We had two bedrooms downstairs, a kitchen, a dining room, and a foyer. I was a pretty good handyman. With some help, I was making the house livable. I put in new carpeting, new locks on the doors, and fixed the windows. The place hadn't really been lived in for a year or more. A little later, Mary Anne got pregnant with our daughter, Samantha. Eventually, the farm house became a 7,000-square-foot finished building.

I was living on a ranch again, but we didn't have any animals. I got some fencing up in anticipation of adding the cattle. Mary Anne became the finance officer for a major car dealership. My divorce had really hurt me financially, so I took baseball coaching jobs to boost my finances and poured the money into the new ranch. Mary Anne and I did not have a fancy wedding. We got married in Las Vegas, and I think the license for Nevada was $100 and another $200 for the ceremony at one of those 24-hour chapels.

I was pitching and coaching in the new senior baseball league and playing in Arizona to make some money. I had a foreman on the ranch. Mary Anne was working, taking care of Raymond and the baby. Then Mary Anne had a terrible automobile accident. It was in December, not long after my birthday on the 13th.

It was not clear initially how Mary Anne was. The senior league was shutting down, and I just needed to fly out of Phoenix and get home. The team's manager was Jim Marshall, the old Cubs player, and he got the clubhouse manager to throw all of my stuff together and mail it to Oklahoma. He arranged for someone to drive my Chevy Blazer home for me. I went to the airport and flew home immediately. Driving along a country road about eight miles from home, Mary Anne had been thrown out of the car. The report was she didn't have her seatbelt on.

Mary Anne was the type of person who, if she saw a possum or skunk run across the road, she would swerve to get out of the way. She did swerve, the car tipped over, and she was thrown through the front window. When we talked, she said she couldn't remember why she swerved, and there was no telltale evidence on the road. The tire blew out, and Mary Anne broke her neck and punctured a lung. The doctors performed surgery and took a bone out of her back to repair her neck. She wore one of those halos to keep your head from moving.

Mary Anne was in intensive care for 30 days, and she seemed to be on the road to recovery, but then she got pneumonia.

I spent part of each day on the ranch. I did the chores each morning and then drove to Oklahoma Baptist Hospital. I'd wash her and talk to her. Mary Anne couldn't speak because she had a tube in her trachea, but sometimes she mouthed words. I read books to her. Then I drove home to meet the kids after school or daycare. On January 10, I got the phone call from Jack Lang about being inducted into the Hall of Fame.

I drove to the hospital and told Mary Anne that I had been selected, and she smiled. She was doing pretty well. I flew out of Oklahoma City to St. Louis and went on to New York for the press conference with the other Hall of Fame inductees. When I got back and went to see Mary Anne, she nodded that she was okay. But only two days after I got back, she expired. I just couldn't believe it. They just couldn't get rid of the bacteria. She was only 31 years old when she died.

I was so depressed and sad, and Raymond, who was 11 at the time, suffered more than I did. I took him to a therapist, and I went to the same therapist. It was a very difficult time. Samantha was only about a year and a half old when her mother died. I was down, and everything seemed to be happening in a fog. Friends and relatives kept offering to help with the kids. And right in the middle of everything, I was contacted by an old girlfriend named Cindy Takieddine from California I hadn't seen in years. We met in 1967 and stayed in touch for a while, but hadn't seen each other in nine years. She had read about Mary Anne's death, and an old friend suggested she should get back in touch with me. She wrote a letter to me in care of the Chicago Cubs.

Cindy had been married and divorced since I had last seen her—her husband disappeared in the Middle East. She was a buyer of women's clothes, but was studying law. She came to Oklahoma, and Samantha just seemed to gravitate to her. Cindy was tall and blonde and looked like Mary Anne, and Samantha started calling her "Mommy." I was a mental wreck, and the only thing I wanted to do was help my kids and fix things so Raymond wasn't depressed all of the time. He was having trouble in school for the first time, and Samantha was crying all of the time. Cindy came for a week—separate bedrooms and all—and said she would like to stay longer. Since she helped so much with the kids, I said okay.

I got a new foreman who had a young daughter, and she became our babysitter if I had an appearance to make. The foreman was great. He knew a lot about horses and cattle and loved ranching. I was breeding cattle again. When Cindy came to Oklahoma, she was recovering from her mother's death. It seemed she must have thought the situation gave her a chance to start fresh with me. I was focused on Raymond and Samantha. I didn't want to jump into anything too fast.

I was meeting with a support group. Those people had seen their families die in fires or floods or in suicides. They seemed to have had worse tragedies than me. There was one family where there was a fire and the parents got out and the children died. When they realized what was happening, they tried to run back into the burning house, but the fire department stopped them. These people had been through nerve-wracking things that would just send you over the edge.

After about a year, things seemed to be turning the corner. In the spring of 1992, Cindy and I got engaged, but we didn't set a date. I started to have some doubts. Cindy seemed inordinately jealous. She helped me open fan mail, and I got a lot of sympathy mail from baseball fans after Mary Anne died. She started throwing away letters from women. When I found out, we had some big arguments. Then I got an offer to get back into baseball as a pitching coach again. I accepted the job before telling her.

Two weeks later, while I was taking care of some odds and ends in Guthrie, Cindy dressed Samantha in a fancy green dress and told her they were going to a Christmas party. Then Cindy took off in the car and drove to an isolated road about 30 miles from the ranch where she sealed off the car, attached a hose to the exhaust pipe, and killed herself and three-year-old Samantha with carbon monoxide poisoning.

I was working at the ranch preparing to pick up Samantha at daycare when I got a phone call from the sheriff's office. When he told me about the deaths, I was so stupefied I could not grasp what he was saying. The sheriff drove me to the site of the car to identify the bodies.

That was the saddest thing I ever had to do in my life. Cindy left a suicide note saying the reason she killed herself was my "betrayal," which was accepting the job. And she said she killed Samantha because she didn't want to leave her without a mother. Instead of a family gathering at Christmas that year, we had a double funeral.

We had already bought Christmas gifts for Samantha, and in a daze I went around town returning dolls and toys with intense anger burning in me. I couldn't sleep through the night. I know a lot of my friends worried about me during this period. I put my faith in God and asked Him to help me through this awful time. And I wanted to be there for Raymond.

Being a religious Baptist helped me. My kids kept phoning me and talking to me. I just left it all up to God. Talking things out seemed to help. Raymond had just lost his mother, and he couldn't deal with it for the longest time. An uncle said I should burn down the ranch house because it might be cursed. Instead, I had it blessed, and I stayed there several more years.

One thing that helped me in my darkest hours was getting together with some of my old Cubs teammates. Randy Hundley was starting his Cubs fantasy camp each winter—it has helped keep us friends more than any single other thing. Randy, who always calls me, "Dude," insisted I come. They wanted me to get drunk, but I didn't feel like it, and I sat around talking baseball with Randy, Billy Williams, Ron Santo, Jim Hickman, and Glenn Beckert. That cleansed my mind a little bit.

A couple of years later, Glenn was with me when I hooked up with my third wife, Lydia. Glenn and I did an appearance for a businessman from Chicago in Arizona. He wanted a couple of old Cubs to liven up his booth at a home show. We showed off the models and about halfway through the afternoon two women came through. I leaned over to Glenn and said, "I've seen one of those girls."

It was Lydia. Back in 1970 in spring training, I took her out to dinner as friends—I was married at the time. Well, she and her friend were standing in one corner giggling while I talked to customers. Glenn went up to them and said, "What are you girls laughing at?" Lydia had read an article in the newspaper saying I was going to be at the home show, and she just wanted to see if I was the same old Fergie Jenkins.

We first met in Scottsdale, Arizona, in the Red Dog Saloon. I was with Billy Williams, Byron Browne, and a couple of other guys, and she came in with other girls. I said, "Hey, check out the covey of quails that just came in." I asked her to dance. After we had our dinner, she went off to California and then moved to Las Vegas. When we met again, Lydia had been a lead dancer at the Tropicana Hotel for about 10 years. She wore those giant headdresses. She was on *The Merv Griffin Show*, *The Mike Douglas Show*. She was a terrific dancer.

Lydia and I began dating, and we were together for two years when we got married in September of 1993. Not all my kids wanted me to get married again. Kimberly, the oldest, said, "No, you shouldn't do it." Delores and Kelly were okay with it. I felt there was a connection to Lydia. I also thought it was good for Raymond. Lydia seemed to understand what Raymond was all about. Everybody got on the same page, and Kelly has thawed. Raymond loves Lydia. They talk all of the time on the phone. Kelly calls. Delores calls. The girls and Raymond send Lydia Mother's Day cards. I didn't ask them to do it. They did it on their own.

Lydia and I got married on the ranch. I thought it was going to be a small wedding with about 25 or 30 people. About 150 people showed up. Beck (Glenn Beckert) was my best man.

Everything is good. I have four grandchildren now. Kelly has three kids, and they all live in Chatham, so I see them when I go home. Raymond lives in the suburbs of Chicago, so I see him when I come to town for Cubs business.

I stayed in Oklahoma for 17 years before giving up the ranch. I even stopped wearing 10-gallon hats, though I do still live in cowboy country. But before I moved to Arizona, I put up some special headstones in the graveyard in Guthrie for Mary Anne, Samantha, and Cindy.

24

Coaching Baseball

When I stopped pitching, I started to teach pitching. The second part of my professional baseball career began in 1989 when the Texas Rangers hired me as pitching coach for the Triple A Oklahoma City '89ers. One thing that helped me get noticed was my work in 1987 as pitching coach for the U.S. Pan American Games baseball team.

Accepting the job with the Oklahoma '89ers changed my life. I was fresh off a divorce and giving up my old home in Ontario. So I moved to Oklahoma, at first living in a condominium in Oklahoma City. I still had the desire to ranch and farm, and that led to my purchase of my second ranch in Guthrie. I was an Oklahoman for years after I stopped working for the team.

I felt I had excellent credibility to be a pitching coach. I had won 284 games in the majors. I recorded seven 20-win seasons, six in a row. And my control was terrific. My ratio of strikeouts to walks—3,192 to 997—is one of the best ever. While I had a good fastball, my success was predicated on mastering several pitches and throwing them to the best spots. If a guy's career was built on throwing 98 miles per hour only, it might be tougher for him to teach. What I did could be taught.

I liked showing youngsters the correct way to pitch and to win with their head and arm and how to best use their ability. Toby Harrah was the manager. The Rangers had a bunch of young, promising pitchers. They had potential but needed a little bit of fine-tuning. One of them was Mike Jeffcoat. Another was Bobby Witt. I tried to do my best to straighten them out and prepare them for the big leagues. My job was to polish them.

They had the tools, but we focused on the finer points of pitching. I talked to them about learning what pitch to throw in a given situation, how to waste a pitch when you want to, and how to fake a hitter out. It was a crash course in teaching what pitching is all about. People had taught me how to do that as I was working my way up to the majors, and I was passing on the information.

I worked with Bobby Witt for about two months. He had a long big-league career. He pitched for 16 years and won 142 games. He had a good winning streak when he went back up. He put it all together. Bobby really wanted to learn. We talked all of the time, on the bus, in the clubhouse, on the plane, always about pitching. He didn't like being in the minors. He wanted to win, as every young player does.

When I turned down Pittsburgh, Los Angeles, and Cleveland, I removed myself from baseball for around five years. I felt I could still pitch when I retired, but after I chose not to pursue those opportunities, I was more of a rancher than a baseball person. Some people laughed when they saw me wearing 10-gallon hats, but one thing I did was show horses. You had to dress the part, and that included wearing cowboy hats, Western shirts, and blue jeans. That came with the territory.

When I was younger, I was a fashion plate. There was a place in Pittsburgh where I bought tailor-made suits. At one point, I was a fashion model in Montreal. I was impeccably dressed, and that meant dressing up. I don't know if wearing suits all of the time was a bigger contrast to my baseball uniform or my ranching uniform. I do know you don't have to dress formally on a ranch when you are shoveling cow manure.

During those years on the ranch, I focused on building up the spread and taking care of my family, and I did not think too much about getting back into baseball. My old teammate Toby Harrah started it going, telephoning me when he became manager in Oklahoma City. I thought about it for about a week before I accepted the offer.

Working with young pitchers is different than working with veteran pitchers. Young pitchers are eager, on their way up, hoping to make it to the majors. They want to harness their talent, improve, and show that they belong. With older pitchers, sometimes they have been injured and are back in the minors to regain their rhythm.

In the midst of my work as a pitching coach for the '89ers, I started to play baseball again. A new league started for Senior Baseball. The idea was for it to be like the Senior Golf Tour, where everyone was over 50, only you didn't have to be that old for baseball. It seemed like it would be fun, and it was good for guys like me who hadn't gotten the game out of their systems. It was supposed to be serious baseball, and you couldn't help but harbor at least a glimmer of thought that some major-league team might be teased into calling you for a comeback. The league started in Florida and played one season there. It happened to be a cold winter in Florida, so not only did the frost ruin orange crops, it made for some chilly baseball games.

The second season, the league resumed in Arizona. I was playing for a team called the Sun City Rays. Rollie Fingers, another Hall of Famer, was on that team as a relief pitcher. It was only a few weeks into the season when the owners pulled out. They were losing too much money. That coincided with Mary Anne's accident when I rushed home, and that was the end of my active pitching career.

After two years of doing the job with Oklahoma, I became the minor league pitching coordinator for the Cincinnati Reds. That meant I supervised the pitching rosters of all of the Reds' farm teams. I had about a half dozen teams to follow. They had a team in Billings, Montana, one in Chattanooga, Tennessee, one in Indianapolis. The teams were spread out, and I traveled between all of them.

I charted pitches and watched the young guys. After I saw them throw in a game, I sat down and talked with them. I did that for two years. I started watching young players when they came into Class A ball and followed them through Triple A.

After a game, I picked their brains about why they threw this pitch or that pitch. Did they know who the on-deck hitter was? Thinking is what the game is about, and a lot of young pitchers are just trying to get by on talent.

I advised knowing who the first three or four hitters were at the start of an inning, so there were no surprises. I told them to know what they wanted to throw, regardless of what the catcher called. I watched them, talked to them, tutored them, and then sent reports to the head office.

At that time, the owner of the Reds was Marge Schott, who became very controversial for some of her extreme views and was eventually forced to sell the team by Major League Baseball. She was also famous for being seen in public with her little dog. She always had that dog around the office when I was there. Marge Schott called me from time to time to ask about how so-and-so was progressing. She stayed up with the Reds' draft picks.

The Reds had used a lot of high draft picks for drafting pitchers. They seemed to be taking my advice when I made the reports, so that was satisfying. It seemed as if I mattered to the organization.

But when Cubs general manager Ed Lynch called me and asked if I wanted to go back to Chicago to be the major-league pitching coach for the 1995 season, I was excited. I stayed with the Cubs in 1995 and 1996. That was an odd time in baseball. There had just been the strike canceling the 1994 World Series, and it extended into spring training. There were guys who had signed on just because the regulars didn't go to spring training.

Finally, the labor battle was settled, and the regular players reported. We held a late, two-week spring training. The Cubs had some pretty good pitching with Jaime Navarro, Steve Trachsel, Kevin Foster, Jim Bullinger, and Frank Castillo. I told the Cubs we needed some left-handed pitchers. We had Randy Myers and Bob Patterson in the bullpen. Patterson was the setup man with one or two other guys. Randy ended up doing great as the closer, but we didn't have any left-handed starters.

One of the biggest difficulties major-league pitchers have is losing their spot in the rotation and going more than four days of rest between starts. This might happen because they go on the disabled list temporarily with a minor injury. They lose that regular routine. Now, part of the new terminology in baseball is when people talk about throwing "simulated" games. This is supposed to help a pitcher regain sharpness without actually pitching to live opposition batters.

They are pitching against their own teammates. They're throwing the ball by people just to see the reaction of how they swing at the pitches. It's not a true reading. They're trying to gain arm strength, but they can do that by throwing batting practice, watching how the ball sinks or breaks. It still comes back to the art of pitching weighed against just throwing.

It was fun being back on the Cubs. This made my third time with the organization, but it was a different role. I was no longer a player, but it felt familiar going out to Wrigley Field. In a lot of ways, it was the same, going out to the Friendly Confines early, getting changed into a Cubs uniform. But then I wasn't getting the ball for my turn in the rotation. I watched the rotation, and some of those kids struggled. The only one who didn't was Jaime Navarro. He knew how to pitch.

Steve Trachsel never really liked pitching at Wrigley Field. He didn't like the winds at Wrigley and giving up home runs that the wind helped. Kevin Foster was a real fighter. He didn't have much of a breaking ball and tried to compensate for that. He had a good fastball. During the 1995 season, all of those guys, Bullinger (12-8), Foster (12-11), Navarro (14-6), and Castillo (11-10), won in double figures. Not bad. Myers had 38 saves. Trachsel won 13 games the next year. Jim Riggleman was the manager, but after two years, the Cubs didn't ask me back.

There were times I thought I might like to manage. I investigated the idea a couple of times, but never got really solid encouragement. At different times, I kind of floated my name when there were openings in Arizona, Pittsburgh, and with the Florida Marlins. I got some interviews. But no job materialized. Other times I thought I would like to coach again, not necessarily as the pitching coach, but I have had no feedback on that, either.

When Dusty Baker was manager of the Cubs, I went to spring training and did some work for him. I was psyched up about that. I can still recognize talent. What I saw was the same thing, a lot of young throwers, and not too many actual pitchers. They all threw hard, hard, hard, but they didn't change speeds much. Their location was terrible. But those things can be improved. They can be taught.

It was fun to work spring training, but the 1996 season with the Cubs was the last time I was in uniform full-time for a big-league club.

25

Conclusion

I have a replica of my pitching hand in bronze at home as a souvenir.

A company got the idea to replicate Hall of Fame pitchers' throwing hands in bronze and sell them to baseball fans. My right hand, life-sized, going up the wrist, was molded. First I put my hand in a rubber mold, and then plaster was poured in and formed the hand. It only took 10 minutes or so.

In the bronze, I am wearing my Hall of Fame ring, and my hand is turned upward with the baseball in it. You can actually read "Rawlings" on the ball. I don't know how many were made or if anybody bought them. I've never seen the hand anywhere for sale, but I've got one.

That is probably one of the funkier things I've done in retirement. Actually, I am only retired from baseball. I am not a retired guy who stays home and watches TV and sits in his rocking chair all of the time. I am busy all of the time, it seems, making appearances for Major League Baseball, for charities, or for sports memorabilia shows and activities.

I travel a lot. I travel 100 days a year for charity appearances. In the summer, I play a lot of golf that is part of tournaments or one-day events for charity. It might be for Major League Baseball alumni, it might be for a specific charity, or it might be to raise money for the Fergie Jenkins Foundation Inc. That is based in St. Catharines, Ontario, and since 1999 I believe we have raised more than $7 million for charities in the United States and Canada.

On the foundation brochure, we state the purpose as, "A charitable organization looking to make a big difference" and "serving humanitarian need through the love of sport." Every year, through the foundation, I sponsor a golf tournament. We have raised money for the Boys and Girls Clubs, juvenile diabetes, Cubs Care, the Make-A-Wish Foundation, Habitat for Humanity, and many, many other organizations.

The Fergie Jenkins Foundation began when Scott Bullock, who runs a baseball academy in Ontario, had me come for a fund-raising event. My friend Carl Kovacs asked me if I had ever thought of putting on a charity golf tournament. We have worked closely together, with others, ever since, and we have made disbursements to at least 175 different organizations. We support the Red Cross, cancer research, and the Canadian Institute for the Blind regularly. Also, when I am at banquets, I tell people if they represent a charitable organization and they want our support, to write me a note on their letterhead, and I will donate autographed baseball items for them to auction off.

A large number of my personal appearances are for charity. I go to a lot of places. Sometimes my wife, Lydia, can't believe how often I am flying back and forth to places, though sometimes she comes with me. I really do have a lot of frequent-flyer miles. But if I can go someplace and lend my name to an event for playing golf or help by going out fishing, I'm glad to do it. The fact that I can do that with my name makes me feel good. My number-one fund-raising priority is for cancer research, but if you can make a difference by donating your name or time, it's good to know you can help.

Baseball has grown and matured a lot in Canada since I was a kid. Many people say I am the most famous Canadian baseball player, and I am still the only player from Canada in the Hall of Fame. But there are more Canadians playing all the time and more in the majors. If I can help out organizations that promote baseball in Canada, I always like to do that.

When I was a kid, I became a Queen's Scout. It's a youth achievement award you can earn, and the reward is a ring. I am proud of that ring because it is a symbol of how I learned the lesson of the importance of helping others.

To some extent, three words have summed up my life: dream, ability, and trust. Those were words to live by. Those were three things I needed to get by.

The *dream* part really goes back to when I was a kid and wondering what I would be when I grew up. Once I realized I had some skills, my dream was to become a professional athlete. It took a little bit longer to sort out that I was meant to be a baseball player. Becoming a professional baseball player took hold as a dream, and I worked toward making that dream a reality.

The *ability* part was self-evident. I had to prove that I had the ability to succeed, first to myself and my coaches, and then to the scouts and the Phillies, Cubs, and other teams. The ability was there, but I had to draw it out with hard work.

I had to put my *trust* in my own skills and judgment, that was I doing the right thing on the playing field each time I went out to pitch, but I also put trust in the people who made the decisions and of course in God. As a player, I trusted myself to know what I was doing. I trusted I was going to approach situations properly and handle myself in the right way when I was challenged on the mound. That was an overlap with ability. I had to trust that I could match my ability against Willie Mays, Hank Aaron, and Willie McCovey.

The three words—dream, ability, and trust—are pretty simple, but they applied to different parts of my life over and over again as I got older. They are pretty general, too, but one way or another I always come back to them and how they fit developments I experience in the sports world and the real world.

Some of my trips are personal appearances to make a living by signing autographs. I did a baseball clinic in Europe, in Vienna, in the summer of 2008. I always go to the Hall of Fame induction ceremony, and I go where I am invited by Major League Baseball. The sport brought a lot of guys to New York for the 2008 All-Star Game for a ceremony because it was the last year of the old Yankee Stadium.

Every so often, the Cubs invite me to Wrigley Field to throw out the first pitch and lead the singing of "Take Me Out to the Ballgame" during the seventh-inning stretch. I sang in a church choir. I sing in the shower. I sing along with the radio in the car. I can carry a tune, and "Take Me Out to the Ballgame" is only about four verses. The words are easy, so there's nothing to panic about. I've done it five or six times. I enjoy doing it. Some people forget the words and hum it. How do you forget the words?

One thing I don't do very much is go to ballgames just to sit in the stands. I never get to watch more than three or four innings. Somebody is bound to recognize me. They come up to me and ask for my autograph, and that's the end of it. He'll say, "I thought that was you." Then other people come up to me. If I'm invited to watch a game from the press box, I'll go because nobody will interrupt me like that.

When the Cubs offer an invitation, I go. I guess most people think of me as a Cub. I won more games with the Cubs' organization than any other. I won a lot of games for Texas, too, and I get invited back there for events and I go. Not so much in Boston, but sometimes.

I was doing an event in Columbus, Ohio, when the terrorist attacks of September 11, 2001, took place. I was with Jerry Lucas, the basketball star, Bobby Bonds, and a couple of other athletes. We were at the airport, but all airline traffic got shut down. They made the announcement, and then a huge wave of police came running in carrying rifles and riot gear. It was an eye-opening moment. We were able to get our luggage and got a ride back to the hotel.

I went through a round-robin of phone messages, talking to Lydia and to my kids, making sure everyone was okay. I spent the day back in the hotel, watching all of the terrorist reports with Bobby Bonds. Some athletes got out of town by limo, and eventually the only ones left were Jerry Lucas and me. He was a terrific rebounder when he played basketball, and he was known for having a photographic memory. We got to know each other that week.

Every morning, Jerry would call and say, "Hey, Fergie, want to go to breakfast?" We kind of lived at the hotel. We didn't have cars, either, but the hotel had some transportation, and after I ran out of clothing, they drove us to a mall. I bought some underwear and new shirts. When I left, there were only about 30 people on the plane.

I had a golf outing in New York on September 26, and I went, but a lot of the American athletes canceled. The promoter got some Canadian athletes to fly in. The whole United States was afraid.

Thinking back on my pitching career, I was lucky in some respects. I had the right type of body for a pitcher. I was long and lean. I had a rubber arm. I was loosey-goosey, and I never had an arm problem. I was a good hockey player and basketball player, but baseball was the right sport for me. When you reach the level in a sport that I did, making it to the Hall of Fame, a lot of fans tend to think it was all God-given ability. That's part of it, but it is hardly the whole truth. Those fans never saw me running in the snow on the golf course, chopping wood, or using that sledge hammer, or even the time I spent learning in winter ball.

Sometimes it seems everyone thinks they can play baseball in the majors because they played Little League. Every father thinks they've got a big-league ballplayer in the household. When I first started, it took guys years to work their way up from the minors. The people who advanced put in the hard work and won. And I had good control. I didn't get promoted because I struck guys out. I got promoted because I didn't walk guys.

At various times, I have said that baseball is easy and life is hard. Baseball is not easy in terms of making it to the top and staying there. It is easy compared to the tragedies and setbacks I have had in my personal life. Compared to having people close to you pass away and having a three-year-old daughter die, baseball is easy, and real life is very hard. I never experienced anything on the baseball diamond as difficult as recovering from the deaths of Mary Anne and Samantha.

I never forgot where I came from and where I grew up. Chatham is a place still close to my heart. I don't live there anymore, but I visit regularly. When I go back to Chatham, I stop at a florist and buy some flowers, then go out to the gravesites of my mom and my dad. They are buried next to each other. I sit there and talk to them for a while.

Over the years, I have had four tattoos etched onto my body. They are for me. You can't see them when I am wearing street clothes. They're mostly around my shoulders. They are tattoos that remind me of my mom and my family and my religion. Most people get tattoos to be seen, but mine aren't seen. They're private.

One reason I am asked to do so much work for charity is because I am in the Baseball Hall of Fame. Once that honor is placed next to your name, it is permanent. It elevates your status. I had no idea that it would mean so much. It is forever. When new players are elected to the Hall of Fame they don't realize how much it's going to affect their lives. It changes your life. It puts more prestige with your name. In a way, it makes you better than you were.

I have been chosen to serve on the Veterans Committee of the Hall of Fame that votes on players who may have been overlooked. I can think of several deserving people who really should be in the Hall of Fame, from my old teammate Ron Santo, to Buck O'Neil, who managed the Kansas City Monarchs in the Negro Leagues, and who kept the stories of the old black players alive. Buck was the first African American coach in Major League Baseball, too, with the Cubs. In 2008 the Hall of Fame unveiled a new statute of Buck O'Neil at the induction ceremonies, and they plan to give out a special award in his name.

If my being in the Hall of Fame can help other people, I am going to do it. I tell people baseball is the best game in the world, and I loved pitching. Every fourth day, I had the chance to go out on that field and show my ability. Yes, there have been hard times in my life, but there have been so many great times and great experiences I never could have imagined baseball would provide when I was growing up in Chatham.

That first tattoo I got said, "Trust in God." And I have.

Sources

The material for this book was gathered primarily from personal interviews with Ferguson Jenkins.

Other material was obtained from the National Baseball Hall of Fame research library files, the *Baseball Encyclopedia,* and the Chicago Cubs 2008 media guide.

Ferguson Jenkins previously collaborated in the publication of three books that also provided information. They are:

Jenkins, Ferguson and Dave Fisher, *Inside Pitching* (Chicago: Henry Regnery Company, 1972).

Jenkins, Ferguson and George Vass, *Like Nobody Else: The Fergie Jenkins Story* (Chicago: Henry Regnery Company, 1973).

Turcotte, Dorothy, *The Game Is Easy, Life Is Hard* (St. Catharines, Ontario, Canada: Peninsula Press, Ltd., 2002).

About the Author

Lew Freedman is the author of 35 books. A former sportswriter for the *Chicago Tribune, Anchorage Daily News,* and *Philadelphia Inquirer,* Freedman has won more than 250 journalism awards. He and his wife, Debra, live in the Chicago area.

Index